THE ROCKY MOUNTAINS

CREST OF A CONTINENT

THE ROCKY MOUNTAINS
CREST OF A CONTINENT

J.A. KRAULIS

TEXT BY JOHN GAULT

Facts On File Publications
New York, New York • Oxford, England

Front jacket Mount Hector, Banff National Park, Alberta.

Back jacket A small brook makes its way through moss and equisetum in a valley forest.

Pages 2–3 The Continental Divide, the eastern boundary of British Columbia, rises a mile above Lake O'Hara and Mary Lake.

Page 4 Indian paintbrush, willow herb and arnica blossom amid boulders.

The Rocky Mountains
Crest of a continent

Copyright © 1986 by J.A. Kraulis

Library of Congress number: 86-45572

ISBN 0-8160-1604-6

Photo Credits

All photographs are by J.A. Kraulis with the exception of pages 33, 34–35, 50–51, 144 (below), by Patrick Morrow, and pages 100 (above), 113 (below), 160, 180–181 by Linda Kuttis.

Design: Marie Bartholomew
Typesetting: Compeer Typographic Services Limited
Printed and bound in Italy

10 9 8 7 6 5 4 3 2 1

CONTENTS

PREFACE   9

TIME AND STONE   11

WATER AND ICE   73

LIFE AND PLACE   133

APPENDIX   193

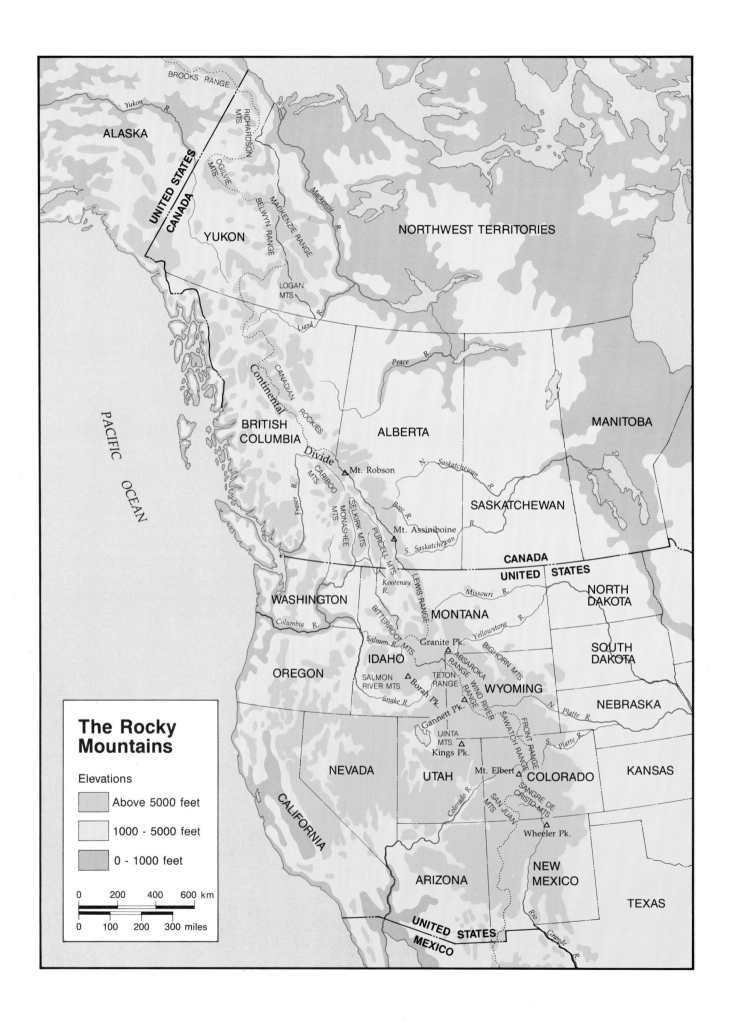

The Rocky Mountains

Elevations

Above 5000 feet

1000 - 5000 feet

0 - 1000 feet

| 0 | 200 | 400 | 600 km |

| 0 | 100 | 200 | 300 miles |

ALASKA

BROOKS RANGE

Yukon R.

RICHARDSON MTS.

OGILVIE MTS.

SELWYN RANGE

MACKENZIE RANGE

Mackenzie R.

YUKON

UNITED STATES

CANADA

LOGAN MTS.

Liard R.

NORTHWEST TERRITORIES

PACIFIC OCEAN

CANADIAN ROCKIES

Continental

Divide

BRITISH COLUMBIA

Peace R.

ALBERTA

MANITOBA

Mt. Robson

CARIBOO MTS.

Fraser R.

MONASHEE MTS.

SELKIRK MTS.

N. Saskatchewan R.

SASKATCHEWAN

Bow R.

Mt. Assiniboine

S. Saskatchewan

PURCELL MTS.

CANADA

UNITED STATES

Kootenay R.

LEWIS RANGE

Columbia R.

WASHINGTON

Missouri R.

NORTH DAKOTA

MONTANA

Yellowstone R.

BITTERROOT MTS.

Salmon R.

Granite Pk.

SOUTH DAKOTA

IDAHO

ABSAROKA RANGE

BIGHORN MTS.

OREGON

SALMON RIVER MTS.

Borah Pk.

TETON RANGE

WIND RIVER RANGE

WYOMING

Snake R.

Gannett Pk.

N. Platte R.

NEBRASKA

UINTA MTS.

Kings Pk.

SAWATCH RANGE

FRONT RANGE

S. Platte R.

NEVADA

UTAH

Mt. Elbert

COLORADO

KANSAS

Colorado R.

SAN JUAN MTS.

SANGRE DE CRISTO MTS.

CALIFORNIA

Wheeler Pk.

ARIZONA

NEW MEXICO

UNITED STATES

MEXICO

Rio Grande R.

TEXAS

8

PREFACE

Few geographical features so conspicuously mark the Earth's surface as do the Rocky Mountains. Yet as prominent as the Rockies are, they remain vaguely defined. Various encyclopedias offer differing opinions on where this chain of rugged peaks begins and ends, and no less an authority than the *Encyclopaedia Britannica* has changed its mind on the matter in recent editions.

The problems of definition are twofold. First, the geological makeup and history of the more than one hundred ranges that may be included in the Rockies is so varied and complex that there is no single aspect which applies to all of them. Furthermore, dramatic new discoveries have revealed that the earlier, static geological picture of western North America is very incomplete and in some ways incorrect.

The second problem in defining the Rocky Mountains has been ignored by almost all writings about them. It is a problem of semantics. The American and Canadian definitions differ hugely. In the official national atlases of Canada and the United States, the outlines on maps showing the limits of the Rocky Mountains do not match at the border. Canadian geographers use the term ''Rocky Mountains'' in a more specific, narrower sense than their American counterparts. If the Canadian definition were to be projected southwards, the Rockies would end in central Montana. Geologically, the Canadian definition would exclude almost all of the American Rockies. On the other hand, if the American definition of the ''Rocky Mountains'' were projected northwards, it would take in, among others, the Columbia Mountains (the Purcells, Selkirks, Monashees and Cariboos) which, as most Canadian schoolchildren know, are west of the Rocky Mountain Trench and are therefore definitely not a part of the Rockies.

In a book of this kind, it seems reasonable to follow the broader definition of the Rockies throughout. Hence the Columbia Mountains are included, as are ranges continuing north of British Columbia. Many American authorities consider the Brooks Range in Alaska to be the northernmost extension of the Rockies, and so in the absence of consensus, this book includes the Brooks and follows the interior, Rocky Mountain portion of the Western Cordillera from Alaska to New Mexico. It constitutes a glorious series of ranges which, while not among the highest in the world, are among the most beautiful, whatever name one calls them.

Mount Hector, the highest summit east of the Bow
River in Banff National Park, Alberta, rises beyond
the tilted strata of the Front Ranges.

TIME AND STONE

In itself, Mount Hungabee in the Canadian Rockies is not a special mountain. It does form part of the Continental Divide, that height of land separating the watersheds of the Pacific and Atlantic oceans. But that does not make it in any sense unique. It is not the highest peak in the Canadian Rockies, nor is it the most formidable. But from the top of Mount Hungabee, you can see endless mountains flowing beyond the horizon – a frozen, angry sea of stone. The imagery is inescapable. It suspends the certain knowledge that not too far beyond the horizon, the whitecapped waves of 1,000-million-year-old rock will dwindle and disappear. It suspends the certain knowledge that this sea is far from frozen, that on a time scale incomprehensible to humankind, it is as violent and unpredictable as the great Pacific which lies well beyond its western edge. It is a glimpse of the eternal.

That is the magic of these Rocky Mountains, and it is not confined to Mount Hungabee or to any single peak or chain of peaks. The Rockies may change in definition, and in configuration and certainly in name as they tower out of the Earth along a twisted line from Alaska to Mexico. But the magic is always there, wrapping itself around the senses.

The Rocky Mountains, like every feature on the surface of the Earth, had a beginning and will have an end. It requires not only an understanding of current scientific knowledge but also an active imagination to comprehend how the Rockies came to be formed and re-formed over millions of years.

The world as we know it began to take recognizable shape about 200 million years ago, when its total landmass (or nearly all of it) was crowded together in an equatorial supercontinent called Pangaea. Pangaea – ''all the land'' – was not the first supercontinent, and it will probably not be the last. But if we had been there 200 million years ago, watching from the Moon, we would have been able to see Pangaea breaking up like ice in the spring. The floes would have seemed vaguely familiar, resembling today's six continents. The locations would be wrong, of course, but if we had been able to stay long enough, we could have watched them moving into their present locations, propelled by forces bubbling up from the molten sea on which our planet's surface floats. How do we know this? Because the process continues.

It is worth noting that as recently as the 1950s the notion of drifting continents, the division of the Earth's crust into moving "plates," was simply unacceptable to many scientists. But like every bright schoolchild who ever stared at a map of the world, there were others as long ago as Francis Bacon in 1620, speculating on how well the Old and New World continents could be fitted together. In Bacon's time, however, the prevailing theory was that the Earth had been shaped by a series of sudden catastrophes, including of course Noah's Great Flood. Whatever might have been believed elsewhere in the world, or whatever past civilizations might have discovered about their planet, the "science" of the seventeenth-century European Christian was still well bound to theology. But evidence that the shaping of the Earth involved the action of slow-moving forces on great land masses had already begun to appear in that self-same century. Fossilized primitive sea creatures, discovered in landlocked rock formations, prompted British scientist Robert Hooke to speculate about how land then above the sea must have once been below it. He even went so far as to theorize about the self-generating properties of the Earth over centuries. But he would be ignored, as would others over the next 250 years who put forward any tectonics theories.

In the 1960s, however, the evidence became overwhelming. Much of the change in understanding would arise out of sophisticated new scientific techniques, involving computers and satellites (which tracked the movement of landmasses). As well, new methods of dating the Earth were developed; highly sophisticated argon and potassium dating systems pushed us closer to discovering the "true age" of the planet. Much knowledge would also derive from current observation of the planet's behavior, the absence of any activity to speak of in the middle of continental plates, and the incredible flurry of activity at their edges. We have learned how to listen to the Earth, and to interpret its growling changes. New techniques were perfected for establishing the age of Earth and Moon rock more precisely: the oldest Earth rock so far discovered is about 4,100 million years old. Techniques were also perfected for determining where and when new rock was formed in the ocean ridges. Fossil remains, ancient clues to the fact that the Earth was not always as we see it now, corroborated the plate tectonics/continental drift theories and led back to the supercontinent, Pangaea. In the early 1970s, for example, fossilized primitive sea creatures were discovered in rocks high in British Columbia. This is not remarkable in itself, and might conceivably support other theories, but what is remarkable is that those tiny fossilized remains have been found in only three other places in the world – Japan, China and Indonesia. They are an estimated 250 million years old, strongly suggesting that the creatures were once pretty much in the same place at the same time – the time of Pangaea when, incidentally, both vegetable and animal life were already well established on the surface of the planet.

Finally, the arrival of satellite tracking and computerized model-building all but confirmed the restlessness of the Earth. So in less than twenty years of revolutionized geology – and especially in geophysics, one of its subdisciplines – a fringe theory became the prevailing theory.

To understand how the western mountains came into existence, we must sweep eastward, over the ancient core of North America – the Precambrian Shield – and halfway across the Atlantic Ocean. A mountain range, the Mid-Atlantic Ridge, wends down the full length of the ocean. It was formed, and is still forming, along a "crack" or "seam" in the planet's crust. Molten materials from the mantle spew up along this crack – the largest of a series of such cracks worldwide that divide the Earth into seven large plates and dozens of small ones. These plates, averaging sixty miles thick (thinner where they are formed in the seabeds, thicker by far where they underlie land) are constantly in motion, pulling away from one another, crashing together, slipping under, riding over.

The Mid-Atlantic Ridge began a division of the Earth's plates, splitting the New World off from the Old, wedging the plates apart at a velocity of about one inch a year. As the rift widened, from Pangaea to the present, so too did the Atlantic Ocean. Some day it will force the North American continent right into the eastern shores of Asia.

If that seems impossible to believe, consider how far North America has already travelled in the past 200 million years – a mere one-fiftieth of the Earth's existence. North America's old eastern mountains and Europe's old western mountains were once indisputably part of the same range.

As North America swung northwestward, its leading edge functioned more or less as a giant bulldozer blade, scraping and lifting offshore sediment that had been deposited on heavier, sinking undersea plates over hundreds of millions of years. The continental plate then ended roughly where the eastern slopes of the Canadian Rockies now begin. The future Rocky Mountain States would ride atop this edge as well. Present-day Idaho and Nevada, California, Oregon and Washington would be picked up along the way. So would Mexico, British Columbia and Alaska.

As the older plates themselves slid under the blade, anything that rode above them stuck to the leading edge. That included islands, submarine plateaus and mountain ranges, and even small continents. As one might expect, the pressure on the leading, above-sea edge was enormous. Great chunks were chipped off and then lifted up on top. And that, in combination with the sediment scraped off the overridden plates, formed the first mountains on the west coast of what was becoming North America.

As the continent of North America was moving westward (about 90 million years ago) at about two inches a year, three things of note were taking place. Along the coast, sedimentary material from the overrun plate was plastered against the old edge of the continental plate, forming an early version of the Coast Ranges of California. In addition, the edge of the North American plate was being further fractured by the confrontation, and thrust eastward in a series of folds that form the western edge of a shallow inland sea. Finally, the edge of the disappearing plate was melted in the lava sea, creating sufficient pressure to open up a range of volcanoes on the surface of the plate; among other ranges, it formed the first Sierra Nevada. In short, three different types of mountain ranges were being constructed at the same time. But not the Rockies. In fact, a series of ranges scraped up along the leading edge would rise and be washed away before the Rockies would put in their explosive appearance.

Between 65 and 45 million years ago, a series of plates began to arrive from the southwest. Created by a volcanic trench deep in the South Pacific, they were on an oblique collision course with the western edge of North America, fracturing the continental plate itself, vertically, horizontally and at every angle in between. From this elemental collision the Rocky Mountains were born; chunks of crust three miles thick were blasted upward and outward by the pressure and heat of a well-fueled furnace fifty miles below. The process would continue for the next 30 million or so years, raising the long high snake of mountain ranges that would come to be known as The Great Divide.

By the latest geological estimates, seventy percent of the present continent lying west of the Rockies arrived from somewhere else in the past 200 million years. San Francisco, to cite a well-known example, is actually built on three different rock formations, one volcanic and two sandstone, and all from different, unknown sources.

And the process continues, unabated. On a scale of human time, the Rockies and the various mountain systems that stretch some 400 miles to the shores of the Pacific seem immutable. But the land is still unstable, still engaged in the twin acts of creation and destruction. The hot belly of the Earth still growls. In places the land is splitting along vast deep seams that may one day separate the Earth's crust. A major plate, the Pacific, now grinds north by northwest, from California to Alaska. The line of its advance is the San Andreas Fault. In 1906 that plate lurched sixteen feet in a matter of minutes, to trigger the most disastrous of all the modern San Francisco earthquakes. In 50 million years, it has been estimated, the section of the plate now riding just north of San Francisco may very well be slamming into the southern edge of Alaska. Forces that can shoulder up wedges of solid granite sixty miles thick can also cause it to fall again. And they have. The area that lies between the Colorado Plateau and the Sangre de Cristo Mountains has dropped six miles. The Rocky Mountains may be our symbol of permanence, but there is no permanence here.

If, in geological terms, the Rocky Mountains are relative newcomers, they do provide a vast and inspiring laboratory in which to understand the natural forces that have shaped our planet. The Tetons of Wyoming, for instance, are among the youngest mountains in the system, only some 9 million years old (as compared to a 60-million-year mean age for the Rockies generally). But they are composed, in large part, of some of the oldest known rock in North America, older than the Shield itself. This rock, called banded gneiss and schist (a dark rock often layered with quartz and feldspar) was squeezed out about 2,800 million years ago in an Earth that was still being hammered by meteors. The banded gneiss, layers of exceedingly hard rock sandwiching (sometimes in spectacular fashion) layers of gray, pink or even black minerals, is the dominant rock of the Tetons, especially at the extremities of the ranges.

It appears in the Grand Teton, the highest and most central range, as great blocks frozen in granite, a rock that is younger by some 300 million years. Aside from the wonders of ancient rock, the Tetons also provide a near-textbook example of "fault-block" mountain building. As they were pushed up to the west of a forty-mile-long, virtually straight fault line, the crust to the east of them dropped, creating Jackson Hole. Nobody is certain what forces were at work underground, but the result was a vertical displacement of about six miles – four times the height of the existing mountains. And the rise and fall continues along the Teton Fault, at the rate of about twelve inches every 300 to 400 years.

The fault-block construction of the Tetons is uncommon in the Rockies, most of which were squeezed up and/or wrinkled over by horizontal compression – the collision of plates. It is not, however, unique: the Wasatch and Uinta mountains of Utah, for example, were created in much the same way, and so was the Centennial Range on the Montana/Idaho border, which rose along an east-west fault.

The state of Colorado provides some of the most dramatic examples of the geological variety within the Rocky Mountain system. While three ranges of the Colorado Rockies – the Laramie, the Medicine Bow and the Park – extend up into Wyoming, the true "roof" of the Lower 48 lies completely in Colorado. It qualifies as the "roof" because it includes the more than fifty peaks in the system that tower 14,000 or more feet above sea level, in the Sawatch, the San Juan and the Colorado Rockies ranges. Like the Tetons, the Colorado Rockies are built of basement rock – albeit 1,000 million years younger – various granites, gneiss and schist. Like the Tetons, these Rockies are fairly recent arrivals, probably no older than 5 to 7 million years.

In the southwest corner of Colorado lies an amazingly different terrain. Here is a miniature Sahara, 10,500 acres of sand dunes, which crest in 600-foot waves to the foot of the Sangre de Cristo Mountains on the east. The Great Sand Dunes may one day be the stuff of future mountains, compressed into sandstone over the millions of years to come. Or the sand may all be washed away by some future planetary whim.

The Sawtooth Range of Idaho is aptly named. Some of the peaks are so pointed that there is barely room for a person to stand. Unlike some of the Colorado Rockies, which are so flat-topped that aircraft could land on them (one pilot of a small aircraft did make a successful emergency landing on Mount Sherman), the Sawtooths look as if they were born only yesterday. Geologically, they were.

Yellowstone is *in* the Rockies, tucked in the northwest corner of Wyoming and spilling over a little into Idaho and Montana. But it is not *of* the Rockies. It appears to have its origins thousands of miles deep in the planet. The Yellowstone landscape conjures up a time when the Earth was not yet middle-aged, when its surface was heavily pockmarked with gigantic seething cauldrons spitting up steam and boiling mud and molten rock. It is one of the magical places in the Rockies, perhaps the most magical of them all. The surface features of Yellowstone, the oldest national park in the world, are spectacular. Its mountain ranges may not compare with the Tetons to the immediate south, but Yellowstone is over four hundred thousand acres of natural (almost preternatural) wonders. Old Faithful, which erupts more or less hourly with 13,000 gallons of steaming water, is the most famous of at least two hundred geysers in the park. Mammoth Hot Springs, with its elegant limestone terraces, is one of several thousand hot springs. Steam hisses, or roars, up from the Earth. Mud pots bubble ominously, like volcanoes in miniature. Yellowstone resembles a vast stove, with all its burners turned to high.

Much of Yellowstone sits in the crater of a gigantic, now inactive volcano, with a mean diameter of more than thirty miles. Less than ninety yards below the surface, temperatures of 400 degrees on the Fahrenheit scale have been recorded, frigid in comparison to what lies farther below.

When Yellowstone becomes an active volcano, as it has done at least three times in the last 2 million years alone, its destructive power is inconceivable. This may be scientific apocrypha, but it has been guessed that during one of its eruptions, it exploded a mountain range the size of the present Grand Tetons. During another eruption (and this is not apocryphal), the floor of the crater suddenly dropped one mile, and the volcano threw out from 100 to 200 cubic miles of molten materials; ash fell as far away as California, Texas and Saskatchewan.

Yellowstone, it should be noted, is due to explode again, and the floor of the crater, the Yellowstone Plateau, has begun to rise at a quickening rate. When it last erupted, it did so with about one thousand times the power of Mount St. Helens at its peak of violence. But the violence with which it erupts is only part of its power – Yellowstone is not a normal volcano. It is the current location of an active ''hot spot,'' one of about twenty in the world (the Hawaiian Islands have been and are being created by a similar phenomenon) and the biggest of them all.

To even begin to understand hot spots one has to visualize a kind of laser source originating in perhaps the very core of the planet. Here and there, around the globe, in no discernible pattern, it fires beams surfaceward, drilling through layer after layer, including the plastic mantle of magma on which the plates ride, and finally through the plates themselves. The plates move, but the ''laser beam'' remains stationary. The North American plate began to ride over the Yellowstone hot spot between 45 million and 65 million years ago. The laser beam began to cut upward through the sixty miles of basement rock plate, leaving behind a string of extinct volcanic islands that now underlie the Coast Ranges. As the North American plate shifted west by southwest, the stationary beam cut a swath underneath it – and eventually above it – passing under Oregon and into Idaho where, about 15 million years ago, it hit the surface with a colossal bang to form the Snake River Plain. Its last major eruption, the last of the three that created Yellowstone, was only 500,000 years ago. And there were minor eruptions as recently as 75,000 years ago. When Yellowstone erupts again in 100,000 years or so, if its once-every-600,000-year ''habit'' continues, the hot spot will be northeast of where it is today. And given its present ''course,'' in a million years it should be somewhere under Montana.

Unlike the southern half of the Rockies, where many of the mountains are made from hard granitic rock, gneiss and schist, which was lifted or exploded out of the belly of the Old Continent, the mountains to the north in Montana, Alberta, British Columbia and Alaska tend to be made from sedimentary rock such as sandstone and slate. This rock was never cooked in the furnace beneath the planet's surface. It was created by pressure, created from dust, particle to particle, beneath the ancient seas. Layer upon layer built up on the seafloor over the millennia – sand, silt, clay, gravel – and shells from the primitive creatures of that sea, which would eventually compress into limestone. The very weight of the sediment helped to squeeze it deeper into the floor of the continent. The lower layers fused into rock – sandstone, shale and limestone and quartzite first – and the rock layers began to build upward, as soon as there was sufficient weight and pressure from above.

When the collision of plates began in the area that was to become the Rocky Mountains, the old sea bottom was thrust up into the sky. Gigantic chunks of sedimentary rock were forced up at the fault lines, grinding and scraping over themselves, landing upright or on their sides, even upside down. In the case of Montana's Glacier National Park, whole ranges slid for distances of up to thirty miles. Entire mountains were sheared off their original bases and now sit upon much younger rock. In many areas of the Canadian Rockies, the subterranean pressure that folded the rock layers like cake dough ultimately shattered those layers, sending up great contorted slabs.

To the west of the Canadian Rockies, across the famed and still-mysterious Rocky Mountain Trench, lie the Columbia Mountains, which by some definitions are not technically part of the Rocky Mountain system. But because they rose out of the Old Continent, they have good reason to be included. Geologically, they are very different from the Rockies. There is some sedimentary rock in the four main ranges – the Purcells, Monashees, Selkirks and Cariboos – but the dominant rock has come up from the basement. If the Rocky Mountain Trench were merely a river-cut or glacier-carved valley, it would not explain why the geological division between the Columbias and the Canadian Rockies is so distinct. What seems almost certain is that the Trench is a major continental fault, a split that runs for thousands of miles. There is some evidence of this: the Columbia ranges, it appears, have shifted several hundred miles "northward" in relation to the Rockies, which is in keeping with the observed movements of land along the west coast of North America. Here, as in the Rio Grande area of the American Southwest, the Old Continent does seem to be breaking up. It has, after all, happened before, and it's happening elsewhere even now.

While the Canadian Rockies end in name high in British Columbia, they continue, at least in terms of sedimentary composition and marine origin, up into the Yukon as the Mackenzie, Selwyn and Richardson mountains. The Brooks Range, which parallels the northernmost shores of Alaska, might also be included in our geological definition of the Rockies. It was once believed (and still is in some quarters) that the Brooks Range swung over, counterclockwise, from the Canadian Arctic; but there is new evidence that it arrived from plates that rode the margin of the Old Continent.

If our journey through the geological history of the Rockies has seemed oversimplified, remember that the path is cut from scientific knowledge and speculation that is no more than a quarter century old. Much more waits to be discovered. What is certain about the Rockies is that they have a capacity to challenge not only the scientists, but also those of us who have experienced their power. They take us back to an earlier and more elemental age when our planet was being shaped. And they remind us of the awesome force and the impermanence of the land beneath us.

Pages 18–19 The view north from a frost-broken summit above Kindersley Pass in Kootenay National Park, British Columbia.

Left The Garden of the Gods below Pikes Peak, Colorado, was formed by the erosion of vertical layers of sandstone, which were originally upturned during the raising of the Rockies.

Above Stupendous cliffs carved from granite during the Ice Ages surround the headwaters of Arrigetch Creek in the Brooks Range, Alaska.

Left Dawn touches the top of War Bonnet peak in the Cirque of the Towers, Wind River Range, Wyoming.

Above A boulder of quartzite shines in a timberline meadow in the northern Cariboo Mountains, British Columbia.

26

Pages 24–25 Its profile readily recognizable from far away, Chief Mountain in Glacier National Park, Montana, is seen here from the prairies near Cardston, Alberta.

Left A rainbow arcs over Mount Rundle, one of the best-known landmarks around the town of Banff, Alberta.

Above Best known as the location of Old Faithful, Upper Geyser Basin in Yellowstone steams with scores of other geysers, fumaroles and hot springs.

Right Scalding runoff from the crater of the inactive Excelsior Geyser cascades into the Firehole River at Midway Geyser Basin, Yellowstone National Park, Wyoming. Algae thriving on the sides of the channels give them their unusual color.

Pages 28–29 Snow whitens the Great Divide and the basin of Lake Oesa, set in a sanctuary of three-thousand-foot-high walls in Yoho National Park, British Columbia.

Above Clouds wreath the ramparts of Castle Mountain, Banff National Park, Alberta, one of the most distinctive mountains in the Rockies.

A September snowfall blankets the boulders at timberline above Hidden Lake in the Sawtooth Range, Idaho.

Above North of the Arctic Circle in the Yukon, the treeless Richardson Mountains escaped glaciation during the last Ice Age, despite their location in a cold climate.

Left Steam rises off Grand Prismatic Hot Spring, the largest hot spring in Yellowstone National Park.

Right Spacious, colorful tundra stretches towards Mount McGrew in the Tombstone Range of the Ogilvie Mountains, Yukon.

Pages 34–35 Late evening sun fires the Tombstone Range.

Opposite A dangerous, shifting place, an icefall on the Bugaboo Glacier in the Purcell Mountains, British Columbia, is a maze of leaning, sculptural seracs.

Above A snowfall has dusted the travertine terraces at Mammoth Hot Springs in Yellowstone National Park.

Left Winter brings light, dry snow, the kind much prized by skiers, to the peaks above Little Cottonwood Canyon in the Wasatch Range, Utah.

Overleaf Looking west from above timberline on Trapper Peak in the Bitterroot Mountains, Montana. Only lichens and scattered patches of grasses and herbs grow amid expanses of sharp, frost-shattered rock.

Above Cloud shadows play across the alpine tundra of the Endlich Mesa and the Needle Mountains, part of the San Juans of Colorado.

Right Deposited by westerly winds at the foot of the Sangre de Cristo Mountains, the Great Sand Dunes are the highest in North America.

Opposite High, fast-moving cirrus clouds sail over the jagged granite pinnacles of the Sawtooth Range, Idaho.

Pages 42–43 Covering a hundred square miles at the foot of the Sangre de Cristo Mountains in Colorado, the Great Sand Dunes are made out of sand blown in from the flats of the Rio Grande River. This sand was originally eroded from the San Juan Mountains far to the west.

Above Wind creates cloud streamers around the distinctive multiple summits of Mount Rundle in Banff National Park.

Above Wreaths of morning clouds surround mountains east of Muncho Lake in the northern Canadian Rockies, British Columbia.

Overleaf The view northwest from Mount Temple in Banff National Park, looking across the Great Divide into Yoho National Park at sunrise.

Above The Goodsirs, the highest peaks in Yoho National Park and among the most impressive in all the Rockies, rise into the clouds in this morning view from Abbot Pass.

Left The setting sun illuminates Yukness Mountain and Mount Biddle in Yoho National Park.

Right Looking north from a small airplane at sunrise near Fernie in the Rockies of southeastern British Columbia.

Pages 50–51 A view across the Selkirk Mountains at sunset, from the Kokanee Glacier, British Columbia.

Above A detail of mudchip breccia in the Grinnell Formation, taken at Comeau Pass, Glacier National Park, Montana. The rock was formed millions of years ago after chips of mud, torn loose by rapid streams, were deposited among accumulating layers of finer sand and silt.

Above The shoulder of Cathedral Mountain is briefly illuminated by the sun during snowy weather in Yoho National Park.

Overleaf A view from the top of a dune in Great Sand Dunes National Monument towards an aspen-spangled valley on the edge of the Sangre de Cristo Mountains, Colorado.

53

Pages 56–57 A pile of great boulders below Jackass Pass in the Wind River Range, Wyoming. Pingora Peak is in the center distance.

Left Snowpatch Spire in the Bugaboos, British Columbia, is a great granite monolith named for the snowpatch halfway up its sheer sides.

Above Sunrise spotlights the high peaks of the Continental Divide, here seen from Abbot Pass on the boundary of Banff and Yoho national parks.

Right Mount Huber, with the mass of Mount Victoria behind it, suffused in evening light, Yoho National Park.

Left Clouds hang in the Rocky Mountain Trench separating the Cariboo Mountains, from which this photograph was taken, and the Canadian Rockies in the distance.

Above The north side of Sentinel Pass in Banff National Park is guarded by numerous impressive rock towers on the flanks of Pinnacle Mountain. In the background is Mount Lefroy.

Left The Ogilvie Mountains in the Yukon contain a large variety of landforms, from sheer spires to the barren, rolling terrain seen here. Fireweed grows in the foreground.

Above The northern Cariboo Mountains and the Raush River, British Columbia.

Overleaf Longs Peak, seen from the bouldered tundra of Trail Ridge, is the highest summit in Rocky Mountain National Park, Colorado.

Above Amid clouds and ragged ridges, a group of small ponds lies at the head of Fall Creek in the Weminuche Wilderness of the San Juan Mountains, Colorado.

Left In vast Gates of the Arctic National Park, north of the Arctic Circle, Alaska, the towers of Caliban catch the light of the near-midnight sun.

Above Looking south from Mount Temple across the peaks of the Continental Divide straddling Banff National Park and Kootenay National Park. Prominent among the glaciated peaks are Mount Fay and Mount Ball, with the pyramid of Mount Assiniboine on the left horizon.

Right A favorite area of serious skiers, mountain climbers and wilderness scenery enthusiasts, the Bugaboos in the Purcell Mountains of British Columbia consist of precipitous granite peaks surrounded by glaciers. Here Pigeon Spire is seen across the col between Snowpatch and Bugaboo spires.

Left The Rockies at sunset rise above the rolling prairies of southwestern Alberta.

Above In contrast to the ancient and hard Precambrian basement rocks of the core and eastern Tetons, Battleship Mountain on the west side is made of softer, newer sedimentary limestone.

Pages 70–71 A small part of the view from the summit of Mount Temple in Banff National Park. The rugged Bugaboos in the Purcell Mountains of British Columbia can be seen sixty miles away on the horizon.

Above Mountain avens carpet a gravelly moraine left by the retreating Southeast Lyell Glacier, Banff National Park, Alberta.

WATER AND ICE

Think about Antarctica. Think of lands buried for thousands of years under billions of tons of ice, buried to the tops of their highest mountains. Or higher – so high that their landscapes are all but featureless, endless frozen deserts of hard glacier ice, dusted lightly with swirling new snow. Now hold the image and superimpose it on the Rockies of today. A few familiar peaks poke through, but they are reference points without any reference. There are no valleys, no foothills, no lowlands, or lakes or rivers or streams. There is only a sea of ice, broken here and there by an isolated rocky summit.

The last time the Rockies looked like that was during the final Great Ice Age, the last of a succession of Great Ice Ages spanning 2 million years. No one is quite sure what spawned these Ice Ages, but the most recent theory focuses on the sudden reduction of the Greenhouse Effect: as a result of increased volcanic activity or meteor bombardment, the Earth's atmosphere was flooded with high concentrations of dust, which reduced sunlight reaching the surface. This killed off many plants and the oxygen they produced. Heat escaped from the planet faster than it could be replaced. The Earth cooled and the polar ice caps spread. Virtually all of Canada and parts of the United States were buried beneath a mile or two of ice, ice that constantly flowed. An unimaginable weight of ice that resculpted and rearranged the world lying buried beneath it. A force of nature powerful enough to grind off thirty feet of basement rock from the surface of the buried continent, and literally carve the Great Lakes out of pre-glacial river valleys. And as fascinating as any of these things is the fact that the last Great Ice Age occurred within human memory; as it reached its zenith, the first known humans to colonize North America were picking their way across the frozen Bering Sea and eventually southward into the heart of the continent. According to one theory, people and animals from the Old World traveled down a corridor that opened between the two great sheets of the last Ice Age – the Cordilleran on the west, and the Laurentide on the east.

Since that time, one hundred centuries or so ago, we have witnessed progressive shrinkage of the ice-cover, a vast lake reduced to a series of shallow puddles. Of the icefields that survive in the Rocky Mountain system, the largest is only eighty-five square miles, and at its maximum, twelve hundred feet deep. This is the famed Columbia Icefield, straddling the Alberta-British Columbia border and the Great Divide, and contributing its still-impressive wonders to both Banff and Jasper national parks. Despite its size and proximity to the highway, the Columbia Icefield is rarely seen except from aircraft, and rarely explored except by mountaineers. Its glaciers are more accessible. There are several visible from the highway near the headwaters of the Sunwapta River. In fact, the Athabasca Glacier is often mistaken for the icefield. But the icefield, above the glacier, is an isolated world, and a dangerous one, even for those who know what they're doing.

In an icefield, or on a glacier where snow fills in and disguises the terrain below, one false step can be the last. Some crevasses can be one hundred thirty feet deep and seventeen feet across at the top. When the surface snow bridge gives way unexpectedly, the effect is similar to a free-fall from a ten-story building. Aside from that, and the ever-present potential for sunburn and snowblindness, an icefield can be mind-numbing: vast, featureless white expanses roughly encircled by white, snowcapped mountain peaks. During clouded-in conditions especially, the icefield experiences a true whiteout. There are no horizons, no reference points; all non-white objects and people appear to be floating in space. A dropoff could be fifteen feet, or it could be fifteen hundred feet. All distance, vertical or horizontal, is impossible to gauge.

The Columbia Icefield produces thirty-odd glaciers, which flow in all directions, wending their way between the highest group of peaks – 10,500-feet-plus – in the Canadian Rockies. And, if the Columbia Icefield and the glaciers it feeds are but mere shadows of their former selves, they are still substantial shadows: one glacier alone, the Athabasca, unleashes 570 tons of geological debris each warm summer's day. Silt, sand, rock and clay emerge from its melting edge, find their way into Sunwapta Lake in southern Jasper, and from there into the Sunwapta River, to be carried, ultimately, into the sea.

If the cause of the Ice Age is unknown, the cause of glaciation is not. Glaciation takes place when more snow falls and stays than melts or evaporates (or sublimates) away. This is most likely to take place when the annual snowfall is high. Every year, to use a metaphor created by an American glaciologist, Robert P. Sharp, each glacier ''works out its budget.'' The budget year encompasses profit (the accumulation of new snow) and loss (the expenditure, or ''wastage'' of old snow). The profits tend to accrue during the winter months at the top end of the glacier, and the losses during the summer months at the bottom end. Continuing with the metaphor, each glacier attempts to balance its budget: if the profits are lower than usual, the glacier reduces its losses by retreating, pulling its leading, melting edge farther up the mountainside. And when losses exceed profits for too many years in a row, the glacier retreats into oblivion. Of course, when the reverse happens, the glacier gets longer and bigger.

Each year at the top end of the glacier, new snow is converted into a more permanent asset, glacier ice, which builds up, layer by layer, for years, decades, centuries, millennia – as long as conditions are right. Sandwiched between these layers, and preserved for future discovery, are windblown dust and pollens, deposited on the surface.

(This layering indicates a glacier's age and some of the local history; counting the layers of a glacier at its top end is the equivalent of counting the concentric rings in a tree trunk – both reveal annual growth and, often, weather conditions.)

Glacier ice is unlike any other; it stands outside most people's experience with frozen water, whether covering a lake or crackling out as cubes from trays. Creation begins with a standard snowfall. Within a few days (or a number of weeks, depending upon temperature, humidity and wind) the infinite structural variety of the snowflakes is lost, replaced by tiny granules of snow. As more snow arrives, it adds weight at the top, compacting the granules of snow ever closer together, squeezing out the air between them. Where there is a summer thaw, meltwater trickling down also contributes to the process, but even without it, the conversion to solid ice continues under the pressure from above. It may take twenty or thirty years of buildup, but eventually each annual layer of snow is compacted and compressed into ice without air bubbles, as hard as rock. Geologists, in fact, consider it to be rock – rock with a low melting point.

But rock, as we know it on the surface of the Earth, does not flow. Glacier ice does, no matter what the temperature. Sometimes it flows very quickly, as Alaska's Black Rapids Glacier did in a 1937 surge, reaching a velocity of 245 feet a day; but, on average, daily movement rarely exceeds 3 feet in the mountain valley glaciers of the Rockies. There is no consensus as to the actual physics of what causes a glacier to start flowing. We do know several things, however: first, the thickness of the glacier ice must exceed 100 feet; second, movement tends to develop first in the middle of the glacier, which is usually the point of lowest friction. The upper layers ride on the middle layers and have no independent motion of their own. The bottoms and sides, unless they have actually disengaged from the underlying rock, are dragged along slowly and reluctantly by the flowing core at the center – and this, obviously, is how glaciers grind and tear away vast chunks of mountainside and hew out their U-shaped valleys. The rock itself becomes the glacier's grinding tool.

Chemically, glacier ice *is* water. And except for a couple of special qualities – it can flow uphill, for example – it continues to act like water. It runs in rivers and streams, following the paths of least resistance. Where the river of ice slides into a natural basin, it spreads out into a lake of ice, filling the basin to its brim, then spilling over to become a ''river'' again. Where the river of ice reaches the edge of a steep cliff, it spills over like a waterfall: in fact, it slides down the surface of the cliff, at an accelerated speed of about ten feet a day, or two or three times that in some conditions. This is the glacier at its most unstable, and therefore its most dangerous. With the ice river fractured by so many crevasses, great chunks will suddenly break off and tumble. Icefalls are as wide as the glacier, and as tall as the cliffs over which they surge, with the highest of them several hundred feet. Where an icefall ends, the river resumes, sometimes with an altered appearance, undulating downward in a series of well-defined waves.

Like all rivers, they continue their search for the sea. And, in one form or another, they ultimately find it. From Greenland and Antarctica, parts of Alaska and the Canadian Far North, they arrive directly as icebergs, shearing off at the edges of the land to float and melt in the currents.

In the Rockies, they convert into water, entering the rivers that lead to the sea. It is worth mentioning that some mountain valley glaciers *do* produce icebergs in mountain lakes. Berg Lake, a body of water 7,380 feet below the summit of Canada's highest Rocky Mountain, Mount Robson, receives glacier ice in its pure form, without any interim melting.

The maul that gouged the Rockies into the rough shapes we see today was made of glacier ice. Even in ranges south of Montana, where the continuous ice cap became fragmented, glaciers left, and still leave, their characteristic signatures – wide, U-shaped valleys (in contrast with V-shaped river valleys) faced with high, nearly vertical cliffs. Where major glaciers once flowed, the valleys are flat-bottomed and networked with "braided" rivers; the soil is rough and gravelly, deposited there as the glaciers receded. Farther up, where smaller, tributary glaciers once flowed, "hanging" valleys remain, often ending now in high, spectacular waterfalls and cascades. And farther up still, where the glaciers first began to form 2-million-odd years ago, are the basins or "cirques," quarried out of the solid rock. Snow-ice buildup began the process, capitalizing on natural depressions and faults in the underlying rock; frost action and erosion took it from there. Once the buildup was sufficient, the lake of ice overflowed to establish a new river of ice; the rock debris hacked and scraped out to form the basin was carried downward and away.

These characteristic features exist throughout the Rockies on both sides of the international border. Glacier National Park in Montana (so named for past glaciers, although half a dozen or so small ones survive) is rightly famed for its hanging valleys and free-leaping waterfalls. For a more spectacular version you have to travel north to Twin Falls and Takakkaw Falls in British Columbia's Yoho National Park. Both falls empty into a U-shaped valley long-vacated by the Yoho Glacier, and Takakkaw Falls, still fed by glacier meltwater, rolls down a cliff-face 1,180 feet high.

Cirques are major contributors to the unsurpassed beauty of the Rocky Mountain systems on both sides of the border. Where they no longer contain glaciers, many have become lakes; and where the lakes have long since filled with washed-down soil and rock, they have become oases of plant, tree and animal life, sometimes featuring a series of small lakes connected by streams. The Canadian glacial lakes are particularly beautiful because they are created by active glaciers. The shimmering turquoise and emerald colors derive from the suspension of an active glacier's finest silt – "glacial flour" – in the lakewaters. The number and size of these tiny particles determine the hue of the water by dictating how it scatters sunlight. There are summits in the Canadian Rockies from which one can look down on both a turquoise *and* an emerald lake without even doing a quarter turn.

Of all these glacial lakes – and there are several hundred – the most famous and one of the most accessible is Lake Louise in Banff National Park, fed by a half-dozen remnants of the glacier that carved its lakebed during the last Great Ice Age. The most impressive, the Victoria Glacier, flows down from the 11,365-foot Mount Victoria, which dominates the backdrop to the southwest. Lake Louise is a striking greenish blue and a favorite of photographers.

The difference between the glacial features of the American and the Canadian Rockies has been determined in part by temperature. Canada's more northerly location has meant a longer and greater exposure to the effects of glaciation. Since mean annual temperature depends as much upon altitude as latitude, it makes sense that ice buildup was greatest highest in the northernmost mountains. The exception appears to be the Richardson Mountains in the northeast corner of the Yukon, which was spared in all the glaciation periods; on the other hand, the St. Elias Mountains (not part of the Rockies) in the Yukon's southwest corner are still heavily iced over. Only in the Canadian ranges of the Rockies system do the low, glacier-built valleys still contain glaciers, though they have been drastically foreshortened. The longest, flowing out of the Columbia Icefield, is the Saskatchewan and it is only six miles long. At its fullest glory, the Athabasca Glacier flowed out for sixty miles, filling the whole valley beyond where the town of Jasper now nestles. Today it is just over three miles long and is receding at the rate of some forty feet a year.

Although glaciation in the American Rocky Mountain system followed a different pattern, the effects of glacier ice were similar. In the Colorado Rockies, the evidence of size and extent of glaciers from the last Great Ice Age remains in the shapes of the canyons and valleys, and in their moraines – ridges of rock and silt left behind when glaciers recede. During one and perhaps both of the very early Ice Ages, valleys were filled with glaciers up to half a mile thick. The largest of these glaciers rolled through the Colorado Rockies for almost twenty miles. And, higher up, are the cirques, the basins carved and quarried by the glaciers out of mountain rock.

It is interesting to note, however, that as recently as 7,500 years ago – the end of the last Great Ice Age as far as the Colorado Rockies are concerned – there was not one glacier of any sort left clinging to the ''roof'' of the Lower 48. Until about thirty-eight hundred years ago, the Colorado Rockies were glacier-free. The snowline was above the summits, and the timberline, the highest point at which trees will grow, was significantly higher than it is now. Then the climate cooled again. In the Canadian Rockies, receding glaciers began to rebuild on their much-diminished bases. In the Colorado Rockies, the glaciers of today were born. They never became very big, no longer than a mile, but on the eastern and northern facing cirques, where the headwalls shut out much of the sun, there was at least a measure of rebirth. They have waxed and waned throughout the intervening years of what has been called the Little Ice Age, a period which, supposedly, is almost over. Within that period, glaciers existed as far south as Santa Fe, New Mexico, but today only a few are active even in the Colorado Rockies. Their tongues (lowest reaches) are pulling back into their heads, or not moving at all.

Another factor that accounts for the existence of glaciers in the American Rockies system is the protective nature of some of the topography. Theoretically, considering the average altitude for summertime freezing temperature in Rocky Mountain National Park, glaciers should not exist there. Summers are too warm and winter snowfall too light for glaciers to sustain themselves. But winter snow bounces off high cliffs and drops into the upland valleys below, accumulating to sufficient depths to keep glaciers viable – with summer help from those same cliffs, which cloak the valleys in permanent shadow.

Still, the glaciers that survive in Rocky Mountain National Park in Colorado are engaged in a losing battle. Few are still advancing and most are receding. This is generally true for the six dozen or so glaciers that remain in the American Rockies system, although impressive glaciers do still grow and flow in ranges to the west, particularly the Cascades in Washington, where the annual snowfall is considerably greater.

That losing battle could reverse itself at any time, however. If there is no scientific reason to believe that we are on the edge of another Great Ice Age, there is no scientific reason to disbelieve it either. It is true that there has been quite rapid shrinkage of glaciers in the past 200 years, but that shrinkage has slowed considerably in the past few years. And in the Pacific Northwest, glaciers have begun to grow and move. One fact we do know is that the process never stops – it only modifies or changes direction.

The Great Ice Ages provided the maul that hacked the Rockies into their present shape, but long before the Ice Ages, which are a recent phenomenon after all, rivers were redefining the mountains. In fact, rivers were running across this part of the Old Continent long before there were mountains to shape – running as rivers must from the high country to the low, seeking and/or cutting channels to the sea. As the Rocky Mountains were being thrust up and folded over and shoved along, rivers were already tearing them down again. If water had its way, the Earth would be uniformly flat. All the highlands would be ground off and carried away, all valleys would be filled. If there can be no mountains without rivers, it is also true that there could be no rivers without mountains. Rivers need a slope.

The process begins when prevailing winds pick up moisture from the vast Pacific, carrying it inland across a succession of high ranges. Then the moisture falls, as rain or predominantly snow, in ever-decreasing amounts as the winds sweep eastward. The water begins its descent, seeking out and finding most of the great river systems of North America.

What the Great Divide divides is watersheds. There are several places in Jasper National Park where, theoretically, one drop of rainwater could splatter and its component parts find their way into three different oceans. The part splashing west would find its way into the Columbia River and enter the Pacific in Oregon. The part splashing east would enter the North Saskatchewan, be borne along into the Nelson, spill into Hudson Bay and sweep around Ungava to the Atlantic. The part splashing northeast would dribble into the Mackenzie River to enter the Arctic Ocean at Tuktoyaktuk in the Northwest Territories. There are many peaks along the Great Divide from which one can see rivers flowing in different directions. For example, from Homestake Peak in the Colorado Rockies, one can see contributing sources of two of America's great rivers – the Colorado and the Arkansas. The former empties into the Gulf of California, and the latter enters the Mississippi, eventually spilling its mountain lake water into the Gulf of Mexico.

Most of the water that flows down from the Rockies begins its stay there as snow, building caps and icefields and glaciers through the winters and setting up conditions for spectacular springtime thaws. In the Rockies, as in all mountains, spring arrives from the bottom up, inching its way from full bloom on the valley floors to the ever-wintry snowpacks at the summits, unleashing the torrents as it ascends. Only when it reaches the high snows, the source of about seventy-five percent of the water that is produced in the Rockies, do the torrents attain full volume. The high snowpack is the source of virtually all the major rivers.

The first phase is short but explosive. A heavy melt or a heavy rain moves with enough speed and force to leave its first gullies visibly and measurably deeper than they were before the flooding began. The roiling waters next find their way into more established channels as the mountain slope diminishes. These streams tend to have a permanent year-round flow – greater, of course, in the warm months – and move through steep, V-shaped valleys, producing turbulent rapids and waterfalls. If one of these streams finds its way into a basin, say one carved out by a long-ago glacier, a lake will be born; and immediately it will begin to die, choked with rocks and sediment carried down from above.

Eventually the white water and cascades disappear and the meltwater that emerged just below the snowpack flows steadily as a river, widening its bed rather than deepening it. Its valley here is U-shaped, and the slopes to either side are much more gradual, grassy and even treed. The erosive action of the water hasn't finished, however: as the river seeks to straighten itself, soil is washed from its outward banks and redeposited on the inner ones. Then, finally, the river slips into and through the foothills and finds the bottom lands, where its meanderings grow longer and more leisurely.

The great rivers of the Rockies have played essential roles in the earliest European explorations. Sir Alexander Mackenzie (who would one day have a major river named after him) breached the mountain wall in 1793 by way of the Peace River – the only river in Canada that actually passes through the Rockies. Twelve years after he reached the Pacific, on behalf of the fur-trading North West Company, an American expedition led by Meriwether Lewis and William Clark did the same – by following the Missouri to one of its three sources, traversing the high passes of the Bitterroot Mountains, picking up the Snake River on the other side, and turning left into the Columbia at its juncture with the Snake.

The mountain rivers, washing down the debris from the high country, also exposed the riches of the Rockies – gold, silver and copper – that would draw the miners, suppliers and settlers into the West at a wildly accelerated rate. And they would also supply the most valuable commodity of all – water. The Great Plains of the United States and the Prairies of Canada, for example, can only survive because of the mountain-source rivers that cross them. Rainfall in the flatlands is far too slight to support agriculture and the cities that have grown up.

And finally, it is the rivers that carve out routes to the far-distant past, to epochs when there were no Rockies. The Arkansas River, which meets the Mississippi River on the border between their namesake states, begins its journey in a lake 11,100 feet high up the eastern slope of Homestake Peak. Called Tennessee Creek, it plunges downward two or three miles and joins other streams to form the headwaters of the Arkansas in a valley called Tennessee Park. The valley was visited by glaciers, once or more than once, but it actually predates them. The Arkansas River Valley, which begins just south of Tennessee Park, is almost thirty times older than the first Ice Age. It was created when the first

Rockies were slowly born, between 65 million and 45 million years ago. And it still displays evidence of that upheaval.

The Arkansas River continues southward, roughly paralleling the Great Divide. Finally blocked by the Sangre de Cristo Mountains, the Arkansas turns abruptly eastward. Only the massive Front Range of the Colorado Rockies stands between it and the Great Plains now. The land is foothilled but, in comparison, relatively flat. In the absence of true mountains, the Arkansas creates them – by carving its own valley progressively deeper into sedimentary rock, exposing on its near-vertical cliffsides a whole history of the land when it lay beneath the sea. By the time it reaches the Royal Gorge, almost two hundred feet wide and one thousand feet deep, it is no longer just cutting through the soft sedimentary rock, it is carving through granite, the same hard pink granite that forms much of the Front Range, twenty miles away.

Once through the Royal Gorge, the Arkansas is out of the mountains, having passed the near-straight line at the eastern foot of the Front Range that marks the Rockies' beginning and end. The geological river tour does not end here, however. Having moved through the New Rockies and the Old Rockies, the Arkansas now confronts the Ancient Rockies – or what's left of them. They were formed some 325 million years ago and, under the forces of erosion, were ground flat about 150 million years later. They were washed eastward, grain by grain, and compressed into sandstone and shale, a bed for the sea to come. Here, between mountain and plain, the Arkansas River moves through a series of sandstone and shale ridges rising as high as 240 feet. They were, and are, a side effect of the rise of the towering Front Range block, 60 to 70 million years ago. Beyond the ridges, the Arkansas slips into the vast flatlands, seeking the Mississippi, the Gulf of Mexico and the Atlantic. The great mountains are behind it now, as ancient as its history. But it carries them with it always.

Opposite A waterfall at timberline above Bourgeau Lake, Banff National Park.

Pages 82–83 Icebergs calved from the melting Cavell Glacier float in the shadow of the awesome north face of Mount Edith Cavell, Jasper National Park, Alberta.

Above The glare of sunlight accentuates the patterns in freshly formed ice on a pond.

Right Whitebark pine, glacier-polished rock and small pools enhance Alaska Basin on the west slope of the Teton Range, Wyoming.

Overleaf Monte Verita and Warbonnet Peak reflected in Baron Lake at dawn. Cradled in impervious granite basins formed by glaciers during the Ice Ages, alpine lakes are very numerous in the Sawtooth Range, Idaho.

Left A substantial river of meltwater flows from an ice cave at the toe of the Southeast Lyell Glacier in a remote part of Banff National Park.

Above An October thunderstorm brews to the west of snow-covered Pikes Peak, Colorado.

Pages 90–91 Columbine Lake in the Vallecito Basin, San Juan Mountains, Colorado, lies high above the trees at over twelve thousand feet. In the center distance are Organ Mountain and Amherst Mountain.

Left Seen from the slopes of Mount Hector, Mount Balfour and the Waputik Icefield rise beyond Hector Lake, one of the largest lakes in the Canadian Rockies.

Above Not yet frozen, a pond below Mount Cramer in the Sawtooth Mountains, Idaho, contrasts with a landscape whitened by an early September snowfall.

Right The majestically glaciated peaks of Mounts Lefroy and Victoria constitute the famous backdrop for Lake Louise, Alberta.

Pages 94–95 Once gouged and scoured by glaciers, the Alaska Basin in the Teton Range is an environment of weathered timberline trees, polished granite and numerous small ponds.

Above Pingora Peak and Lonesome Lake are part of the scenery created by now-extinct glaciers in the Cirque of the Towers, Wind River Range, Wyoming.

Above A gorge carved by Avalanche Creek in Glacier National Park, Montana.

Overleaf Icebergs in August fill a small lake below the Bow Glacier in Banff National Park.

Above Fresh snow commonly softens the hard edges of bouldered alpine country as early as September, but usually doesn't last, disappearing for a while during Indian summer in October.

Right Summer is always short in alpine country. Snow several feet deep buries everything in this April scene at Jonas Pass, Jasper National Park; it will not melt away for another three months.

Opposite A silted glacial river from the Peyto Glacier enters and mixes with the waters of Peyto Lake, Banff National Park.

Overleaf The Snake River winds across the plain at the foot of the Teton Range, which includes some of the most impressive peaks in the American Rockies.

Left Victoria Falls descends in picturesque steps below Ringrose Peak on the Continental Divide, Yoho National Park.

Above The Kicking Horse, the main river through Yoho National Park, runs relatively clear in the spring, when it is not yet swollen with the milky, silted meltwater from glaciers.

Right Voluminous even at the onset of winter, twice as high as Niagara and located in a unique geological setting, Lower Falls in the Grand Canyon of the Yellowstone, Wyoming, is one of the most spectacular waterfalls in the world.

Pages 106–107 One of the numerous wandering channels of the North Saskatchewan River, which braids its course along a broad, flat glacial valley in northern Banff National Park.

Left Beyond Lake O'Hara, Mount Owen is visible between Mount Schaffer and Odaray Mountain in the Rockies of British Columbia.

Above The Vowell Glacier, seen here from Northpost Spire, flows amid dark granite towers in the dramatic Bugaboo region of the Purcell Mountains, British Columbia.

Overleaf The matterhorn of Mount Assiniboine is the most prominent feature in a beautiful region of the Canadian Rockies that includes Magog, Sunburst and Cerulean lakes, seen here from Nub Peak.

112

Left The brink of Lower Falls in the Grand Canyon of the Yellowstone, Wyoming, is one of the most dramatic places in all of the Rockies. The exploding waters fall three hundred feet surrounded by brightly colored walls of heat-altered rhyolite.

Above The Totem is reflected in a lake surrounded by larch trees in St. Mary's Alpine Park, Purcell Mountains, British Columbia.

Right A small pond at timberline on Silver Mesa in the San Juan Mountains, Colorado.

Pages 114–115 Whitehorn Mountain and Mount Robson, the highest in the Canadian Rockies, seen at dawn from the Cariboo Mountains, British Columbia.

Above Although not the highest in elevation above sea level, Mount Robson, British Columbia, is indisputably the most impressive mountain in all of the Rockies, rising the highest above its own base, and bearing several glaciers that descend uninterrupted from the summit for one-and-a-half vertical miles.

Right The sun breaks through clouds over the wild, trackless valley of the Raush River in the northern Cariboo Mountains, British Columbia.

Above A cavelike recess frames one of the numerous falls in Johnston Canyon, Banff National Park.

Left Moss thrives along the fringes of a shady forest brook.

Right War Bonnet Peak on the Continental Divide is the backdrop for a small alpine waterfall in the headwaters basin of the North Popo Agie River, Wind River Range, Wyoming.

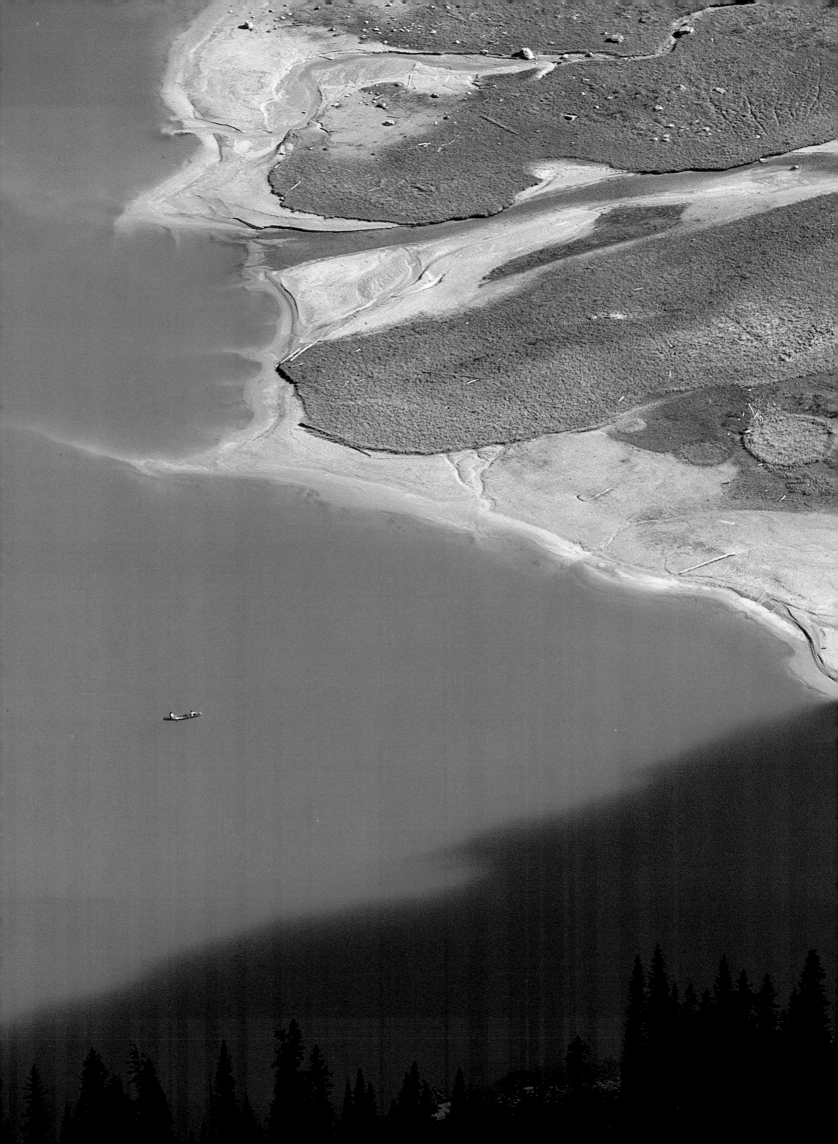

Left A canoe provides scale for this view down onto the west end of Lake Louise, Alberta, taken from the cliff of The Beehive.

Above Indian summer in October sometimes brings such clear, still weather that lakes, such as this one in St. Mary's Alpine Park, British Columbia, remain mirror smooth for several days.

Right The striking blue glacial waters of Lake McArthur are the backdrop for a pair of spruce trees, probably well over a hundred years old, growing at timberline in Yoho National Park.

Pages 122–123 In the arctic climate just below the top of Mount Temple, a large snow cornice lasts year-round. Below are the Ten Peaks in Banff National Park, the rugged ranges of Kootenay National Park beyond these and, on the distant horizon, the Purcell Mountains.

Pages 124–125 A thundercloud expands over Lizard Head Peak and Bear Lake in the Popo Agie Primitive Area, Wind River Range, Wyoming.

Left The Columbia Icefield region has the lion's share of the high peaks of the Canadian Rockies, including Mount Athabasca, Jasper National Park.

Above Sacred Dancing Cascade on McDonald Creek in Glacier National Park, Montana, steps down the layered, broken rock of the Pritchard Formation.

At timberline in the shadow of steep glaciated peaks, Lake Oesa in Yoho National Park remains ice free only, at most, three months of the year.

Above Autumn leaves collect in a small pool at the base of a waterfall.

Overleaf Peyto Lake is one of the many lakes in the Canadian Rockies that owe their beautiful color to the scattering of light by glacial flour, fine particles of silt suspended in the water.

Ferns cover the floor of a dense forest in the Purcell
Mountains, British Columbia.

LIFE AND PLACE

The Indians called it "Ghost Walker" and sometimes the "Cat of God." Early settlers shivered at the sound of its voice, a banshee scream that reverberated through the darkness of the New World night. It was often heard but rarely seen.

Of its many names, the most common today is "mountain lion." But until one hundred fifty or so years ago, the cougar (or puma) was no more exclusive to the mountains than to the forests or plains or river valleys. It hunted wherever the deer were plentiful, and lived wherever it was safe – which, until the Europeans came, was everywhere from the Atlantic to the Pacific. Then, as wave after wave of immigration pushed across the continent, felling the forests and carving up the land, the cougar was driven ever westward. Finally, it took its last refuge in the forbidding high country of the Rocky Mountains.

The same pattern was true – or largely true – for humankind's other major competitors, the wolves, coyotes and grizzly bears, and the bald and golden eagles. We shot, trapped and poisoned our way across the continent, eliminating prey and predator alike, firm in our belief that the supply of deer, elk, buffalo and beaver was infinite – and in our belief that they were put there for us alone. Cougars, wolves, grizzlies and coyotes were our competition, threats to our security. So we killed as many as we could and drove the survivors into the far north, or up into the high mountains. They were safe from us there, at least for a while. The Rockies were too rugged, too cruel and inhospitable for all save a handful of intrepid people.

When the railways came in the nineteenth century, and then the roads, the impenetrable was penetrated. Mining and logging, and much later sports and recreation, came to the Rocky Mountains little by little, range by range, across the cordillera to the shores of the Pacific. Species that had taken refuge in the mountains were again threatened. The threat came with the herds of domestic livestock, grazing the high plains. It rode on the bullets of big-game hunters. It wafted up from poisoned carcasses, left to entice some starving wolf or coyote, or golden eagle or cougar (though that technique didn't work for cougars; they only eat what they kill). At last, toward the end of the century, and just in time, governments recognized the priceless natural heritage of the western

mountains. A series of national parks were created in the American and Canadian Rockies, beginning with Yellowstone in 1872. Parks became refuges, sanctuaries for wildlife. Hunting and trapping underwent more regulation and policing. At various times, various creatures went on a protected list. Programs were created to nurture the truly endangered species back to a stable and viable population, using relocation, captive breeding and winter food drops. A new bargain was struck with nature.

Like the Earth itself, mountains are divided into a series of zones, roughly concentric belts identifiable by temperature, vegetation and wildlife. Distance from the Equator, of course, plays the same role in mountain systems as it does on the flatlands. The Sangre de Cristo Mountains of New Mexico, irrespective of height, will be warmer year-round than, say, the Brooks Range of Alaska, and therefore more hospitable to much larger varieties of life. There are other variables as well: life on the windward western slopes will not necessarily reflect life on the leeward eastern slopes, any more than life on the sunwashed southern exposures will reflect life on shaded northern faces. What is *not* variable has to do with altitude: for each 1,000 feet of ascent, the temperature drops three degrees Fahrenheit. At the top of Pikes Peak in Colorado's Front Range, it is more than forty degrees colder than it is at sea level, all other factors being equal. Life as we know it, and life as we can endure it, ends at the treeline.

Winter is fierce in the high Rockies. It descends from the towering, comparatively lifeless peaks and grinds down the slopes, taking its toll every foot of the way. Foothill pastures may be lush in April, springtime paradises for domestic livestock. But a mile above, the elk and mule deer are starving, struggling through a frozen world in search of grass to graze or leaves to browse. Many will drop from hunger and exhaustion – especially the very young and the very old – before they ever reach the warmer valleys. Spring is a good time for the wolves and coyotes and the big cats, but the gain is often short-term: next year the herds will be smaller, especially following a truly bad mountain winter, and the predators will suffer. Only the strong survive.

Here and there, in parks along the Rocky Mountain chain, we attempt to bend that law. In Grand Teton National Park, for instance, 24,000 acres of land have been set aside to grow food for the resident elk herd. Drops are made in regular feeding areas and the herds have grown and prospered. But as is so often the case when we interfere with nature, there is a downside. When the elk, which are normally loners, crowd together on a feeding ground – and some are now staying year-round – the chance of spreading disease is increased.

Because the mountain summers are short, 150 days at best, and winters all but overlap both the spring and fall, life in the Rockies is like life in the Arctic: highly specialized. Even where there is no summer at all, in the permanent glacier ice of the summits, one form of life finds a niche – its only niche. The ice worm, a cousin of the common earthworm, feeds on pollens left by the wind on the surface snows.

Above the Rocky Mountain treeline virtually all life and growth is compressed into at best a six-week summer, when tourists such as the deer and elk, and their hunters, the cougar and coyote, look for a quick meal. But this high, windlashed world *does* support a permanent population – pikas, hoary marmots, ptarmigans. Each has adapted in its

own special way to the harsh conditions above the treeline. The marmot, a spaniel-sized cousin to the groundhog and woodchuck, eats frenziedly through the brief summer, building up thick layers of fat; then when winter arrives, it burrows down and truly hibernates. The pika, a short-eared, rat-sized relative of the rabbit, does not hibernate. It harvests grasses in late summer, collecting a bushel or more, cures them in the sun, then lives off its stores all winter. The ptarmigan, a smaller member of the grouse family, forages year-round; in the absence of competition from other birds in winter, the ptarmigan has the snowfield to itself, treading on feet feathered into "snowshoes" from one exposed bud to the next. There is one more large creature (as opposed to a number of insects, including grasshoppers) that makes a more or less permanent home high above the treeline. The mountain goat, common to the Canadian Rockies and as far south as Montana and Idaho, survives the winter on mosses that grow on the otherwise desolate rocks. This three-foot-high antelope (it is not, in fact, a goat) may shelter itself just below the treeline when the weather turns especially vicious, but its security from predators lies above, in the summits where it leaps nimbly from narrow ledge to tiny outcrop. Rocky barren summits are truly what the mountain goat was built for: its cloven hooves are hard-edged and can chop their own footholds in the ice; and between the hard toes are soft pads that grip rock surfaces like suction cups.

Animal life of any sort anywhere is predicated on vegetable life. Even the ice worms must nourish themselves on windblown pollen. And vegetable life relies on at least a semblance of a growing season – a summer, however short, and, of course, soil.

Above the treeline, a natural cycle exists that creates food for the few animals and birds able to endure at such altitudes. The lichen is, for most purposes, the first real link in the food chain, and a major and indispensable contributor to the manufacture of soil in which other plant life will root and flourish. Lichen is not a single plant but a symbiotic pairing of a fungus and an alga. The job of the fungus is to absorb moisture and minerals from the rock and pass them through to the alga, as well as to anchor each pairing. The alga produces the food and supplies the fungus with the carbohydrates it needs to survive. As lichens spread, they create and colonize new worlds, assisting in the breakdown of rock into soil (a chemical process that complements erosion) and nourishing that soil with their dead remains. Mosses appear next, and then grass, and so on. Over a period of centuries, the lichens and their successors, along with wind and rain and glacial ice, crumble the solid rock of mountains into a medium that can support more advanced varieties of flora. This, in turn, opens the way for more varieties of fauna, which, by way of their droppings as well as through aeration (by worms, burrowing insects and burrowing animals like the gopher), further enrich the soil for even larger and more varied plant and animal life.

Obviously the soil at the foot of mountains is infinitely richer and more abundant than the soil at the top. The soil above the Rocky Mountain timberline is tundra, no different from that in the High Arctic. Tundra, a Finnish word meaning "land without trees," occurs in varying shallow depths in the highest meadows, valleys and crevices. Frozen as many as ten months out of twelve, it is soil of wretched quality, and except for certain grasses, it can support no plant life that grows in the lowlands. But, amazingly, it does

support life above the treeline – often a multicolored profusion of life. Rushing to grow and reproduce in the short respite that separates winters, alpine flowers suddenly roll out in carpets of purple and yellow, delicate mauves and hardy rich reds. As with their animal, bird and insect cohabitors, the plant life of the alpine tundra obeys the law of natural selection as it is most rigorously applied. The rich colors of the blossoms, like the rich green of the leaves, are designed to absorb the precious heat of the sun, rather than reflect it. Plants tend to bunch tightly together, huddling for warmth; the temperature within such a cluster can in fact be fifty degrees higher than in the surrounding earth. They also tend to lie low to the ground, supported by short, wiry stems, all in defence against winds that can gust close to two hundred miles per hour. Some – the saxifrage family for example – conquer the elements by swift action: growing, flowering and dropping pollen in a mere five days. Others, such as alpine phlox, grow very slowly, adding a leaf or two a year; one no larger than a tennis ball has likely been growing for more than a century. At least two out of three of these alpine flowers could grow nowhere else.

All survival above the treeline, and much of the survival just below it, depends on specialization. In the higher zones of the Rocky Mountains, the food chain is extremely fragile. If any one of the links is broken, the whole ecosystem could come unstrung. But, fortunately, life above the timberline is protected by inaccessibility and climate. The marmots and the pikas and the handful of other rodents that eke out life on the near-barren summits need only fear the golden eagle, North America's largest winged hunter, and the carnivorous contingent of summer tourists – the cougars, bobcats, wolves, coyotes, foxes and bears which foray up from the forests below to partake of the summer harvest.

In the far-northern ranges of the Rockies system, the alpine zone is the only zone. There is no timberline on the north slope of the Brooks Range, because no trees grow that far north. At the southern end of the system, the next zone down – called subalpine or montane – tends to belt the mountains between 5,000 and 9,000 feet above sea level. This is the realm of mountainside forests, dominated by a half-dozen or so species of tree. Here, unlike the alpine barrens, larger plant life can, under certain conditions, establish rootholds. The Douglas fir, for example, succeeds whether the sunlight is good or bad. Along with the other evergreens – trees that evolved to cope with cold, dry weather and gale-force winds – the Douglas firs command the middle zone of the Rockies. The only major deciduous challenger is the tall, slender, trembling aspen, extensive throughout the Rockies on both sides of the international border. When it comes to surviving in nutritionally poor soil, and soil that cannot retain water very well, the firs, pines and spruces are far better equipped. The hard, waxy needle, with its single central vein, is much more efficient than the broad leaf when it comes to processing food and water. It is also less porous, so less is wasted.

The test of any tree's ability to survive is, of course, most rigorous at the timberline itself. The difference between tundra – the land without trees – and the soil that begins to nurture trees is slight. The timberline undulates across the mountain slope; its trees stately and uniform at the lower reaches of the zone, but scattered, flattened and twisted grotesquely by the wind at the top. In spots where the wind is broken, little copses

may form, their trunks huddled close together, branches dipping close to the ground, protecting themselves (and the odd high-roaming animal) from the elements. Depending upon latitude, the world just below the timberline is dominated by one or another of the Engelmann and white spruces, the alpine fir and whitebark pine.

The whitebark pine is one of the toughest trees in the world, a gnarled dwarf that grows in impossible places, splitting up out of what seems to be solid, soil-free rock. In the northern end of its range, in middle British Columbia, it bows to the wind, spreading out supine like a broken hand. At the southern end, in the Sawtooths and the Tetons, it stands stout and proud, as much as three feet in circumference and thirty feet in height. It has become, quite rightly, the symbol of the timberline, etched in all its twisted glory against a backdrop of cold gray rock and crystalline blue sky.

Another tree that has adapted to life at the timberline is the glorious alpine larch. It is a rare tree for a number of reasons. Although it is a conifer, it sheds its needles each fall. It is unique to a small area of the Rocky Mountain system (plus the Cascades of Washington to the west), distributed through a range of about four hundred miles, and then only in widely separated patches. The alpine larch is unusual in that it stands upright, thirty to forty feet high, in a region largely defined by stunted, flattened trees; it copes with the wind by bending to it. It carries the glories of autumn into a world of grays and greens and browns. In September, four short months after the snows have gone (and a few days or weeks before they return) the alpine larch turns saffron yellow. Then the needles fall, to lay a shining carpet on the unyielding landscape.

One animal frequently identified with the timberline of the Rockies, from the southern United States to northern British Columbia, is the bighorn sheep, and, northward into Alaska, its cousin, the Dall's sheep. The bighorn is not exclusive to the timberline, but it is singularly adapted to survival in the highest, harshest places. Nevertheless, the male's distinctive curling horns, averaging more than three feet in length, came very close to dooming the bighorns in the last century, when trophy hunters assaulted the Rockies in droves. The competition from domestic livestock in the more accessible areas, plus diseases contracted from domestic sheep, further lowered their numbers to the mere 35,000 that still survive today. Dall's sheep, thanks to the remoteness of their range, have largely succeeded in maintaining their numbers – 65,000 to 95,000, mostly in Alaska and the Yukon. In the case of both species, survival is based on exceptionally good eyesight, alertness and a remarkable ability to climb, as well as speed and agility. Adults have virtually no natural enemies in the high country, and while lambs are sometimes grabbed by golden eagles, they are outrunning and outmaneuvering other major predators within a few hours of birth.

As the Rockies descend through the montane forest, and the wilderness comes closer to the human domain, most of the last of North America's big game cling precariously to one of the few remaining strongholds on the continent. From the eastern slopes of the Rockies to the western slopes of the Coast Range, we can occasionally find a truncated version of large North American wildlife as it existed only 200 years ago. The gray wolf, for example, has been virtually wiped out in the continental United States. This wondrous creature, with its highly sophisticated social and hunting organization is, without

question, the smartest animal on four legs. Of all the competitors humans faced in their evolution into the dominant species, the wolf was the most impressive – at least in the northern world. Thus, it had to be suppressed, not just in North America but throughout its global range, which among mammals is still second only to that of humans. Unlike the tigers of India, which were still challenging for dominance as recently as two centuries ago, wolves rarely attacked people (all those myths to the contrary). They were merely good competition for the game animals – deer and elk and caribou and moose and wild sheep. So we killed them by the hundreds of thousands, and forced the survivors to retreat farther and farther into the marginal lands of the mountains and the far north. There may be no more than forty thousand left in all of North America, heavily concentrated in the northwest corner. And even here, when it suits the whim of a government to pander, say, to the elk-hunting lobby, we helicopter in with rifles and poisoned carcasses and kill a few thousand more.

In the absence of wolves in the mountainous American West, the two major predators are cougars and coyotes. They have virtually nothing else in common. The cougar, the New World's second-largest big cat, once roamed both North and South America. It is a prime example of a hunting mammal driven into the hinterlands. Except for a few stragglers spotted from time to time in Florida and Eastern Canada, its range has shrunk almost exclusively to the western mountains of the United States. The coyote, on the other hand, has spread eastward from the mountains over the past two centuries, claiming the wolves' old territories. Half the size of the gray wolf (except where they have interbred) the coyote is almost as smart and, in terms of avoiding people, much better adapted. Where it serves their purpose to operate in packs – a new phenomenon – the coyotes form them. When a mated pair and its offspring are numerous enough to ensure survival, coyotes stay with their traditional social arrangement.

The cougar, on the other hand, is a cat that walks by itself. Once the mating period is over, after a couple of weeks, male and female go their separate ways. As with most cats, save the true lions of Africa and India, the only lasting social relationship among cougars involves mothers and young. And that only lasts until the mother is pregnant with a new litter. Working alone in the high mountain forests, the wild valleys and even desert country, the cougar prevails as the continent's finest hunter. Preying largely on mule deer, the species most common to its habitat, the cougar relies on both power and speed. It can leap more than sixteen feet straight up, for one thing, and while it is not a distance runner, it can match a deer in a short dash. It is also the continent's most humane killer when it lands in the right position, hitting the deer's shoulders and, in the same motion, severing its spinal column with its long, sharp canine teeth, causing almost instantaneous death. And the cougar only kills to eat, rarely more frequently than once a week, which is one of the reasons the Indians also named it "keeper of the deer." No one knows how many cougars padded the forests, swamps, plains and mountains before we began to eliminate them. Now, protected or partially protected through most of their mountainous range, about sixteen thousand survive in the United States.

The bears, both grizzly and black, are perhaps the best adapted to the harsh life of the mountains (except, of course, for the creatures who live there exclusively). Both species

of bear follow a varied diet, which is mostly vegetable. Only twenty percent of what they eat is animal in origin, and much of that is of the rodent variety. In the summertime, for example, the average adult black bear may eat in excess of 200,000 berries a day. As well, the bears do not have to cope with the ravages of winter. While they do not technically hibernate, they achieve a kind of coma sleep which lasts until the babbling of running water above arouses them in the spring. A bear in spring, especially a female who has been nursing cubs for a month or so in the den, emerges as a shadow of her former self; she will have burned off a good one-third of her body weight.

It is hard not to think of a grizzly bear as one of the major predators of the Rockies, considering that the male can stand close to ten feet tall and weigh up to seven hundred pounds (more than twice that in parts of Alaska) and is, without question, one of the most dangerous creatures on dry land. But like the black bear, the grizzly feeds predominantly on roots, grasses and berries. Fish, where available, supplement that diet, as do rodents and small game. But when a grizzly does confront larger game – a moose or caribou or elk – the battle is quite spectacular. And when a grizzly is provoked by a human the results are often tragic, not to mention predictable. Grizzlies, along with their smaller cousins the American black bears (which are not always black, incidentally), are a real threat to people, whenever conditions are right. Despite the continuing efforts of park and wildlife personnel on both sides of the border, people continue to breed familiarity. Once a bear starts taking human handouts, a prohibited but apparently irresistible activity for many tourists, that bear can start demanding human handouts. And once a bear starts demanding, blood may be spilled – first the human's and eventually the bear's.

Today, bears can still be found throughout most of Canada and the United States, with (as one might expect) concentrations in the more remote areas. The grizzly, however, has had its natural range – which is, ideally, wide open spaces – shrunk to the Rocky Mountains and points northwest. Again, it is a familiar story: as the nineteenth century began, perhaps one hundred thousand prowled the western United States. Now there are less than one thousand left in the American Rockies and maybe thirty thousand more in the Canadian-Alaskan reaches of the western and northern mountains.

The last of the continent's great predators survive in these mountains only because most of the continent's last great prey animals also survive in the western and northern mountains. Elk, caribou, moose and mule deer were hunted close to extinction across lower North America in the period between 1800 and 1900. Since that time, thanks to protective legislation, restoration programs and a proliferation of parks and wildlife refuges, most have made respectable comebacks. None of these major browsers or grazers is exclusive to the Rockies. But without the Rockies, a century or so ago, some of these species might well have perished. They managed to hide behind the great rock walls and, along with their predators, wait out the worst. Although each species was decimated by the turn of the century – save perhaps, the caribou, generally speaking a very northern creature – enough remained to provide a viable gene pool. In other words, inbreeding did not occur frequently enough to further doom the dwindling species. Ironically, even that one-ton symbol of our wanton destruction, the plains bison, or

North American buffalo, also survives – at least in its wild state – only in parks in the American Rockies and in Wood Buffalo National Park in Canada. The thousand or so survivors of more than 50 million killed by 1890 have grown to about fifty thousand today. The plains bison, in the Canadian context, was brought in to mingle with its closely related subspecies, the wood bison, which survived the slaughter thanks to its habitat of mountains and woodlands.

Of all the creatures that took to the mountains and the stark valleys and deserts that separate them, the one that most excites the human imagination is not technically wild at all. It is also not a game animal, so that its preservation is of little concern to the powerful hunting lobbies, in contrast to concern for the mule deer, the elk and the moose. And that is why, even in the mid-1980s, the eradication of the magnificent mustang continues to remain a real possibility. By definition, wild horses are *feral*, descendants of domesticated horses that were first reintroduced to North America by Spanish explorers and conquerors in the sixteenth century, and supplemented over time by other runaway or abandoned domestic horses.

Without the protection afforded "wild" animals, the mustang herds were treated as vermin through most of the last hundred years. They were butchered by the thousands for dogfood, shot on sight and left to rot, or poisoned. Boxed into corrals and blind canyons, they died of thirst and starvation. Why? Because they competed with commercial livestock for grazing lands, and thereby offended the ranching lobby, which has many friends in high places. Only in the past twenty-five years, and then with only intermittent success, have counterlobbies formed to save the mustang. Nobody knows how many are left – estimates in the mid-1970s ran from less than thirty thousand to about seventy thousand. The remnants of the millions that thundered over the West 200 years ago now gallop proud and free in only a handful of western states, all of them mountain states.

By the time we began to rethink our role in nature, to understand and accept that we do not and cannot stand separate and aloof from it, we had wrought an inestimable amount of damage. Then our penchant for mindless slaughter gave way to cynical self-interest: if we kill off all the deer today, we won't have any to kill off tomorrow; and if we kill off the wolves and cougars, who will cull out the old and the weak, to keep the herds strong and therefore worth hunting? And now, as we glance forward to the twenty-first century, even that attitude has been largely replaced with a genuine sense of compassion and responsibility. We make room for the big cats and the wolves, the elk and the deer, the bears and the mustangs because we are learning to accept that *they have a right to be there*. We can never restore their world as it was, but we preserve and protect enough of that world to ensure their continued survival.

By the simple fact of their very existence, the Rocky Mountains and the ranges beyond have given us that second chance. When we were at our worst, they sheltered enough of our victims to keep the species we threatened alive. As hard as we tried, we could not sufficiently invade that continent-deep fortress of rock. The Rockies protected our major wildlife from us, and, as it turned out, saved us from ourselves.

A mountain goat relaxes on a rocky ledge. Amazingly adept on precipitous terrain, the animal has been seen in places difficult for even human mountain climbers to ascend.

Pages 142–143 The flower-covered slopes along The Garden Wall in Glacier National Park, Montana, with Mount Reynolds in the distance.

Above A couple of weeks before turning in for its winter sleep, a grizzly roots around in a snowy Yellowstone meadow.

Left Snow-blasted trees on a ridge above cloud-filled valleys in the southern Selkirk Mountains, British Columbia.

Right Unlike its relative, the wolf, which has been relentlessly extirpated from most of the Rockies and the continent, the coyote has thrived in spite of intense human pressure.

Left Purple saxifrage is one of many wildflowers that find sustenance in cracks and small patches of dirt in the alpine environment.

Above Spring and winter seem to overlap, as new snow in September covers blossoming fleabanes in the Sawtooth Range, Idaho. In the alpine environment, summer is but a brief intermission in a winter that lasts two-thirds of the year.

Pages 148–149 Amid a sea of conifers, a line of aspens grows along the bottom of a well-drained gully near Wagon Wheel Gap in the San Juan Mountains, Colorado.

Above A mountain goat billy browses in the Rockies of northern Montana.

The tassled seed pods of western anemones fill an alpine meadow below Mount Hungabee, Yoho National Park.

Left A dominant mule deer buck sports a formidable set of antlers in Waterton Lakes National Park, Alberta.

Above Lichens color a boulder in the Brooks Range, Alaska.

Right Like its larger, more formidable relative, the grizzly, the black bear will eat almost anything, but is primarily a vegetarian, despite its scientific classification as a carnivore.

Overleaf Alpine larch in autumn dress above Lake Louise in Banff National Park, Alberta. In the background are the impressive walls of Mounts Lefroy and Victoria.

Left A plush patch of moss finds a stable plot on which to grow amid numerous stream channels at the rocky, treeless headwaters of the Arrigetch Creek in the Brooks Range, Alaska.

Above Indian paintbrush grows at timberline in the Purcell Mountains, British Columbia.

Right A pair of elk. Often shy and elusive in high country retreats in summer, the animals become more casual about human presence in winter, when heavy snows drive them into traveled and inhabited valleys.

Above The dead but handsome weatherbeaten trunk of an old whitebark pine in the Sawtooth Mountains, Idaho. One of only half a dozen species of tree capable of surviving at timberline in the Rockies, the whitebark in some places grows stout, gnarled individuals of great character.

Right Aspens in autumn gild a mountainside south of the town of Aspen, Colorado. The aspen ranges along the entire length of the Rocky Mountains, the only tree that does so.

Left An aspen grove above the Vallecito Valley in the San Juan Mountains, Colorado. The tree, found the length of the Rockies, grows especially tall and straight in Colorado.

Above A small brook makes its way through moss and equisetum in a valley forest near Banff, Alberta.

Pages 162–163 Surrounded by the pink blossoms of willow herb and other wildflowers, a brook cascades down the slopes below Outpost Peak in Jasper National Park, Alberta.

Above Hardy, resourceful and bold, the Canada jay or whiskey jack is often the only apparent sign of activity in the quiet winter of the wild Rockies.

Right Dwelling at timberline where winters are very long, hoary marmots spend most of their lives in hibernation.

Opposite On a warm summer day, a bighorn ram rests on a snowbank in Glacier National Park, Montana.

Opposite A profusion of lichens grows in the Brooks Range, Alaska. In the background are the jagged Arrigetch Peaks, named for an Eskimo word meaning "fingers of the hand extended."

Above With all the trees around them bare, a few aspens cling to their leaves below Slumgullion Pass in southwestern Colorado.

Left Aspen and lodgepole pine near the junction of the North Saskatchewan and Howse rivers in Banff National Park.

Pages 168–169 Mosses and arnica flourish in the moist coolness of Akaiyan Falls in Glacier Basin, Glacier National Park, Montana.

Above Weathered wood of whitebark pine and new snow are part of the many textures of timberline.

Right Bison graze in the broad meadows of the Yellowstone Plateau, one of the few places where the creatures still roam wild and unfenced.

Left Cotton grass thrives in a wet, boggy section of the meadows below The Towers in Mount Assiniboine Park, British Columbia.

Above A mule deer doe pauses at the edge of the forest in Jasper National Park.

Right A deep carpet of lichen covers the tundra above one of the lakes in the treeless Aquarius Valley, Gates of the Arctic National Park, Alaska.

Pages 174–175 Restricted in range between central Montana and southern Banff National Park, and in habitat to timberline, the unusual alpine larch is a beautiful and at the same time extremely hardy tree.

Above Staghorn lichen grows in a notch of an old, weathered tree trunk in the Bitterroot Mountains, Montana.

Left The antlers of this bull elk, photographed in summer, will grow considerably larger and will lose their velvet by the time of the fall rut in October.

Right Ferns and pink-blossomed willow herb grow in moist gravelled ground in Jasper National Park.

Pages 178–179 Fireweed blankets the floor of a burned-out forest in the northern Rockies near the Liard River, British Columbia.

Above Wildflowers line a brook in the alpine meadows of Kokanee Glacier Park, Selkirk Mountains, British Columbia.

Right A detail of the forest floor at the northern end of the Canadian Rockies near the Liard River, British Columbia.

Overleaf Made of large exposures of red rock called the Maroon Formation and extensively forested with aspen, the Elk Mountains are perhaps the most colorful in Colorado, especially in the autumn.

Left Curious but wary, a hoary marmot pauses at the entrance to its miniature cave among the boulders of an alpine basin, a place into which it can readily scurry to safety.

Above Mushrooms grow on a forest floor matted with conifer needles.

Right Grouse in Banff National Park.

Pages 186–187 A small clump of fireweed illuminates the arctic landscape of the Arrigetch Peaks in the Brooks Range, Alaska. In the distance are Xanadu, Ariel and Caliban, peaks unofficially named by the mountaineers who have climbed the granite cliffs of the region.

Above Arctic poppies thrive in the rolling rocky tundra of the Richardson Mountains in northern Yukon.

Above Growing in many patterns and colors, lichens enliven the stony tundra of the Rocky Mountains.

Overleaf Conifers and aspens in various stages of turning create an autumn mosaic below the Maroon Bells, Colorado.

A mountain goat kid has a less than fifty percent
chance of surviving to adulthood, and since only
one or two are born at a time, the species is very
vulnerable to decimation from hunting.

APPENDIX

PARKS AND WILDERNESS AREAS IN THE ROCKY MOUNTAINS REGION

CANADA

ALBERTA

Banff National Park
Location: S.W. Alberta on the east side of the Continental Divide. Access by road to trailheads and through park.
Size: 1,640,000 acres*
Natural Features: Seven hundred miles of hiking trails through some of the finest alpine scenery in the world. Canada's first and most heavily visited national park. Highlights: Cave and Basin Hot Springs, Lake Louise, Valley of Ten Peaks, Egypt Lakes, Icefields Parkway, a 143-mile scenic drive through the center of the Rockies.

Jasper National Park
Location: S.W. Alberta on the east side of the Continental Divide. Access by road to trailheads and through park.
Size: 2,680,000 acres
Natural Features: Large national park in the Rockies; wide variety of wildlife and beautiful mountain scenery attract over 2 million visitors each year; many glaciers and icefields including the Columbia Icefield.

Waterton Lakes National Park
Location: S.W. Alberta on the Alberta-Montana border. Access by road to trailheads.
Size: 140,000 acres
Natural Features: Waterton Lakes and Montana's Glacier national parks became the world's first international peace park in 1932. Chain of three Waterton Lakes; superb trail system.

Willmore Wilderness
Location: S.W. Alberta on the east side of the Continental Divide. Access by road to trailheads.
Size: 1,130,000 acres
Natural Features: Wildlife include bears, wolves, elk and moose; 160 miles of trails connect with Jasper's trail system.

Other Wilderness Areas and Parks
Ghost River Wilderness Area, Kananaskis Provincial Park, Siffleur Wilderness Area, White Goat Wilderness Area

BRITISH COLUMBIA

Bowron Lake Provincial Park
Location: S.E. British Columbia in the Cariboo Mountains. Access by road to trailheads.
Size: 300,000 acres
Natural Features: A canoeist's paradise of lakes and rivers.

Glacier National Park
Location: S.E. British Columbia in the Selkirk Mountains. Access by road to trailheads and through park.
Size: 328,000 acres
Natural Features: Mount Dawson, 11,123 feet; Rogers Pass, 4,225 feet, splits park; half of park lies above 6,000 feet; more than one hundred glaciers; 100-mile trail system.

*Acreages are approximate.

Hamber Provincial Park
Location: S.E. British Columbia on the west side of the Continental Divide. Access by trail from Jasper National Park.
Size: 60,000 acres
Natural Features: Fortress Lake, a turquoise alpine lake surrounded by mountains and glaciers.

Kootenay National Park
Location: S.E. British Columbia on the west side of the Continental Divide. Access by road to trailheads and through park.
Size: 347,000 acres
Natural Features: Radium Hot Springs, a developed mineral pool and bath; Marble Canyon, a deep gorge with a trail along its rim; Paint Pots, a source of ocher once used by local Indians.

Mount Assiniboine Provincial Park
Location: S.E. British Columbia on the west side of the Continental Divide. Access by trail.
Size: 95,000 acres
Natural Features: Mount Assiniboine, 11,870 feet, ''The Matterhorn of the Canadian Rockies''; most of park is above 5,000 feet; numerous small lakes, notably Lake Magog.

Mount Revelstoke National Park
Location: S.E. British Columbia in the Columbia Mountains. Access by road.
Size: 64,000 acres
Natural Features: Mount Revelstoke, 6,358 feet, road climbs to just below its summit; Miller and Eva lakes and views of towering cliffs and snowfields; western red cedar groves.

Mount Robson Provincial Park
Location: S.E. British Columbia on the west side of the Continental Divide. Access by road to trailheads and through park.
Size: 536,000 acres
Natural Features: Mount Robson, 12,972 feet, highest mountain in the Canadian Rockies; Berg Glacier on the north face of Mount Robson; Berg Lake.

Wells Gray Provincial Park
Location: S.E. British Columbia in the Cariboo Mountains. Access by road to trailheads.

Size: 1,280,000 acres
Natural Features: Five large lakes and numerous small ones (notably Murtle Lake); rivers, waterfalls, lava beds, glaciers and mineral springs.

Yoho National Park
Location: S.E. British Columbia on the west side of Continental Divide. Access by road to trailheads and through park.
Size: 324,000 acres
Natural Features: Twenty-eight mountains over 9,800 feet; Mount Goodsir, 11,686 feet; 26 alpine lakes, including Takakkaw Falls, one of Canada's highest waterfalls.

Other Wilderness Areas and Parks
Bugaboo Glacier Provincial Park, Elk Lakes Provincial Park, Kokanee Glacier Provincial Park, Monashee Provincial Park, Muncho Lake Provincial Park, Kwadacha Wilderness Provincial Park, Purcell Wilderness Conservancy, Silver Star Provincial Park, Stone Mountain Provincial Park, St. Mary's Alpine Provincial Park, Top of the World Provincial Park

NORTHWEST TERRITORIES

Nahanni National Park
Location: western Northwest Territories, near Yukon border. Access by charter air services and by canoe.
Size: 1,160,000 acres
Natural Features: South Nahanni River cuts three great canyons more than 3,000 feet deep through the Mackenzie Mountains; Virginia Falls, more than 300 feet high; numerous hotsprings, caves and other unusual geological wonders.

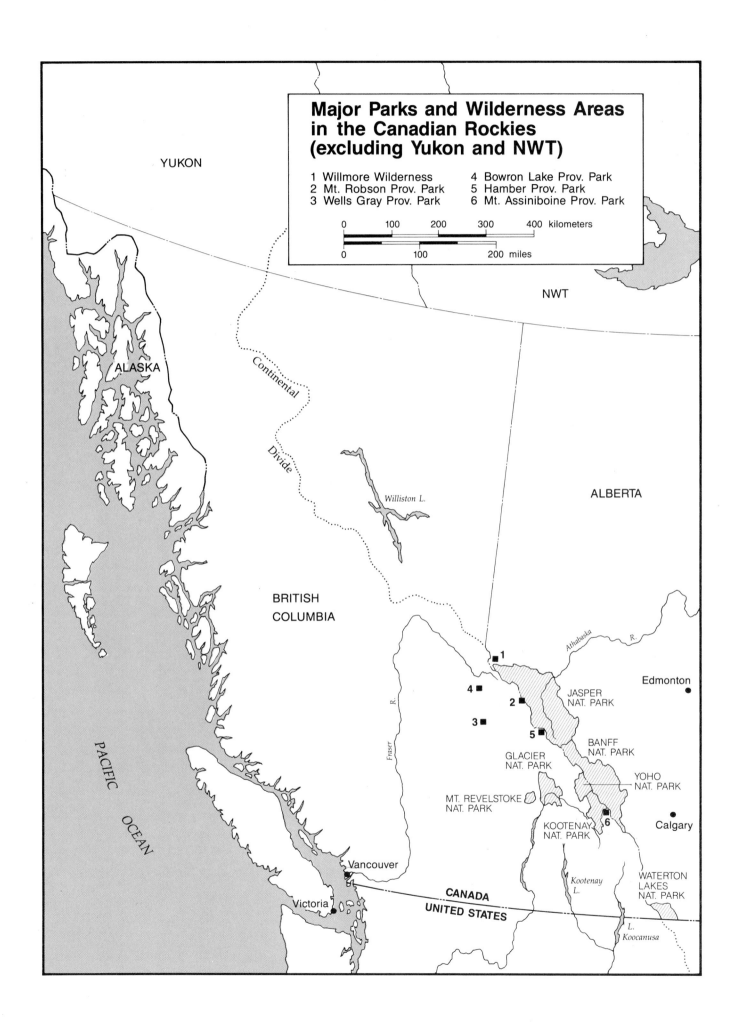

Major Parks and Wilderness Areas in the Canadian Rockies (excluding Yukon and NWT)

1 Willmore Wilderness
2 Mt. Robson Prov. Park
3 Wells Gray Prov. Park
4 Bowron Lake Prov. Park
5 Hamber Prov. Park
6 Mt. Assiniboine Prov. Park

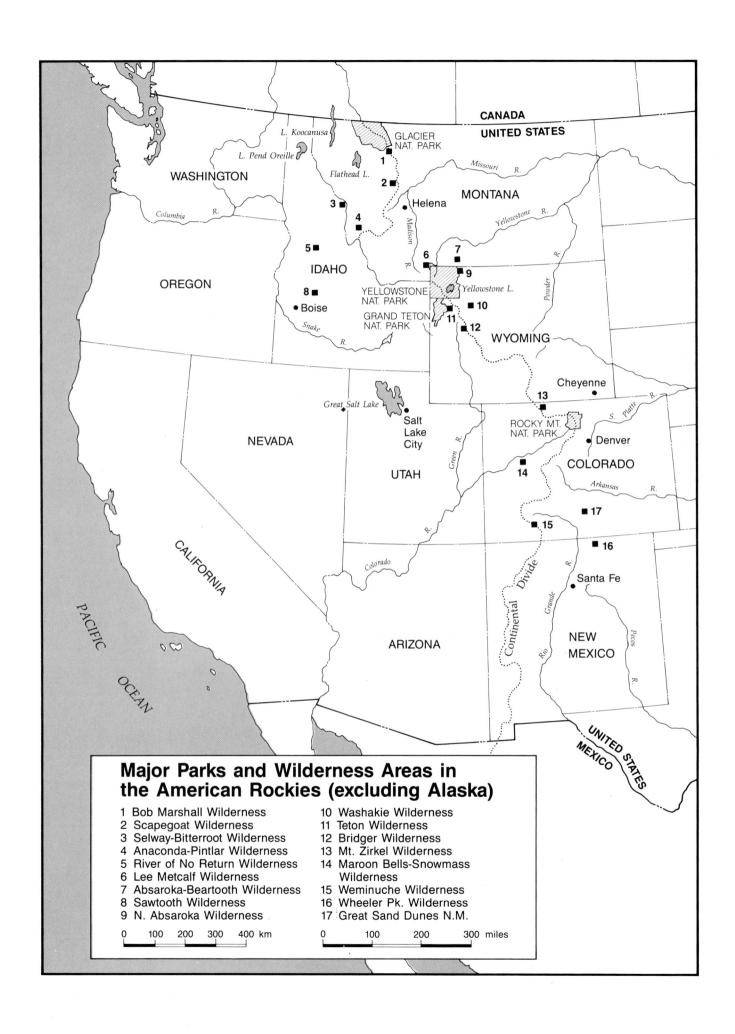

Major Parks and Wilderness Areas in the American Rockies (excluding Alaska)

1 Bob Marshall Wilderness
2 Scapegoat Wilderness
3 Selway-Bitterroot Wilderness
4 Anaconda-Pintlar Wilderness
5 River of No Return Wilderness
6 Lee Metcalf Wilderness
7 Absaroka-Beartooth Wilderness
8 Sawtooth Wilderness
9 N. Absaroka Wilderness

10 Washakie Wilderness
11 Teton Wilderness
12 Bridger Wilderness
13 Mt. Zirkel Wilderness
14 Maroon Bells-Snowmass
   Wilderness
15 Weminuche Wilderness
16 Wheeler Pk. Wilderness
17 Great Sand Dunes N.M.

0   100   200   300   400 km

0   100   200   300 miles

UNITED STATES

ALASKA

Arctic National Wildlife Range
Location: Northeast corner of Alaska. Access by bushplane.
Size: 8,900,000 acres
Natural Features: Calving grounds of the Porcupine Caribou Herd; Lake Schrader and Lake Peters; numerous glaciers and the highest peaks in the Brooks Range, including Mount Chamberlain, 9,020 feet.

Gates of the Arctic National Park and Preserve
Location: central Brooks Range in northern Alaska. Access by charter air services.
Size: 7,952,000 acres; largest national park in the Rocky Mountains.
Natural Features: One of the finest remaining areas of vast, unspoiled wilderness in the world; large populations of moose, Dall's sheep, black and grizzly bear, wolf and caribou; extensive arctic tundra; spectacular sheer granite spires such as the Arrigetch Peaks and Mount Igikpak, 8,510 feet, highest in the central Brooks Range; Boreal Mountain and Frigid Crags (the ''Gates of the Arctic'').

Kobuk Valley National Park
Location: eastern Brooks Range in northern Alaska. Access by charter air services.
Size: 1,140,000 acres
Natural Features: beautiful arctic rivers; the Great Kobuk Sand Dunes, covering 25 square miles and rising 100 feet high; caribou migration routes cross passes in the Baird Mountains in the northern section.

Noatak National Preserve
Location: eastern Brooks Range in northern Alaska. Access by charter air services.
Size: 6,400,000 acres
Natural Features: Noatak River drains the largest mountain-ringed wilderness basin in North America, bounded by the Baird Mountains to the south and the de Longs to the north; extensive wildlife populations.

COLORADO

Maroon Bells-Snowmass Wilderness
Location: N.W. Colorado. Access by road to trailheads.
Size: 174,000 acres
Natural Features: Maroon Bells, a group of famous peaks in the Elk Mountains.

Mount Zirkel Wilderness
Location: N.W. Colorado. Access by road to trailheads.
Size: 140,000 acres
Natural Features: Mount Zirkel, 12,180 feet, and 13 other peaks over 12,000 feet; more than sixty-five lakes; Wyoming Trail offers spectacular views to east and west.

Rocky Mountain National Park
Location: N. Colorado. Access by road to trailheads and through park.
Size: 262,000 acres
Natural Features: Rugged terrain, glaciers, canyons, sparkling lakes, many peaks in excess of eleven thousand feet elevation. Highlights: Bear Lake, surrounded by high peaks; Estes Park; Alberta Falls; Longs Peak, 14,255 feet.

Weminuche Wilderness
Location: S.W. Colorado. Access by road to trailheads.
Size: 401,000 acres
Natural Features: Needle Mountains, an area of pinnacles, several over fourteen thousand feet; Rio Grande Pyramid, 13,081 feet, a popular landmark for climbers.

Other Wilderness Areas and National Monuments
Big Blue Wilderness, Collegiate Peaks Wilderness, Eagles Nest Wilderness, Florissant Fossil Beds National Monument, Great Sand Dunes National Monument, Hunter-Fryingpan Wilderness, Indian Peaks Wilderness, La Garita Wilderness, Lizard Head Wilderness, Mount of the Holy Cross Wilderness, Mount Massive Wilderness, Mount Sneffels Wilderness, Powderhorn Primitive Area, Raggeds Wilderness

IDAHO

Frank Church River of No Return Wilderness
Location: N.E. Idaho. Access by road or by chartered airplane to trailheads.
Size: 2.2 million acres, largest designated wilderness outside of Alaska.
Natural Features: The Gorge of the Main Salmon River, more than a mile deep for 180 miles; Bighorn Crags, an area of numerous 10,000-foot peaks; 190 recorded bird species; elk, mountain lion, bear, lynx.

Sawtooth Wilderness
Location: Central Idaho in the Sawtooth National Recreation Area. Access by road to trailheads.
Size: 216,000 acres
Natural Features: Nearly three hundred miles of maintained trails through a rugged mountain landscape. Wildlife include: mule deer, elk, mountain goat, black bear, mountain lion, bobcat, wolverine.

Selway-Bitterroot Wilderness
Location: N.E. Idaho and across the crest of the Bitterroot Mountains into Montana. Access by road to trailheads.
Size: 1,250,000 acres
Natural Features: Hundreds of alpine lakes, small streams and the picturesque Lochsa and Selway rivers.

Other Wilderness Areas and National Monuments
Craters of the Moon National Monument, Gospel Hump Wilderness

MONTANA

Absaroka-Beartooth Wilderness
Location: S. Montana, north of Yellowstone National Park. Access by road to trailheads.
Size: 920,000 acres
Natural Features: Granite Peak, 12,799 feet, highest point in Montana; Beartooth Range, hundreds of lakes and streams, vast cliffs and narrow canyons; Absaroka Range, rich forests, steep rocky ridges, Island and Mystic lakes.

Anaconda-Pintlar Wilderness
Location: S.W. Montana on the Continental Divide. Access by road to trailheads.
Size: 158,000 acres

Natural Features: Forty-five-mile trail traverses serrated mountain landscape of cirques, alpine lakes and snowfields.

Bob Marshall Wilderness
Location: N.W. Montana, south of Glacier National Park, on the Continental Divide. Access by road to trailheads.
Size: 950,000 acres
Natural Features: Includes several mountain ranges and three river drainages. Highlights: The Chinese Wall, a 12-mile-long line of limestone cliffs; Needle Falls on the White River; Sphinx Peak, 9,510 feet.

Glacier National Park
Location: N.W. Montana on the Continental Divide. Adjoins Canada's Waterton Lakes National Park to make up the Waterton-Glacier International Peace Park. Access by road to trailheads and through park.
Size: 1,013,000 acres
Natural Features: Over seven hundred miles of trails through a hiker's paradise of glaciers, lakes, hanging valleys, lush vegetation and a wide variety of wildlife. Highlights: Avalanche Basin, a natural amphitheater with 2,000-foot-high walls; Many Glacier, spectacular alpine country; Going-to-the-Sun Highway, a popular route through Glacier.

Lee Metcalf Wilderness
Location: S.W. Montana, northwest of Yellowstone National Park. Access by road to trailheads.
Size: Bear Trap Canyon unit, 6,000 acres; Spanish Peaks unit, 78,000 acres; Taylor-Hilgard unit, 140,000 acres; Monument Mountain unit, 34,000 acres.
Natural Features: Wildlife range, numerous trails, glacial cirque basins with small lakes; Gallatin Peak, 11,015 feet.

Scapegoat Wilderness
Location: N.W. Montana, south of Bob Marshall Wilderness, on the Continental Divide. Access by road to trailheads.
Size: 240,000 acres
Natural Features: Spruce, fir and lodgepole forest, alpine meadows and high mountains; largest herd of bighorn sheep in Montana.

Other Wilderness Areas and Wildlife Refuges
Cabinet Mountains Wilderness, Gates of the Mountains Wilderness, Great Bear Wilderness, Mission Mountains Wilderness, Moiese National Bison Range, Ninepipe National Wildlife Refuge, Red Rocks National Wildlife Refuge

NEW MEXICO

Wheeler Peak Wilderness
Location: N. New Mexico. Access by road to trailheads.
Size: 6,000 acres
Natural Features: Wheeler Peak, 13,161 feet, highest peak in New Mexico.

Other Wilderness Areas
Latir Peak Wilderness, Pecos Wilderness

WYOMING

Bridger Wilderness
Location: S.W. Wyoming on the west side of the Continental Divide. Access by road to trailheads.
Size: 390,000 acres
Natural Features: More than thirteen hundred lakes and eight hundred miles of trout streams; Gannett Peak, 13,785 feet.

Grand Teton National Park
Location: N.W. Wyoming. Access by road to trailheads and through park.
Size: 310,000 acres
Natural Features: Soaring Grand Teton Range (Grand Teton, 13,770 feet); Jenny Lake; Signal Mountain (can drive to summit); Jackson Hole, a broad valley favored by elk, pronghorn antelope, mule deer, osprey, bald eagles.

North Absaroka Wilderness
Location: N.W. Wyoming, east of Yellowstone National Park. Access by road to trailheads.
Size: 360,000 acres
Natural Features: Trout-filled streams, foot trails, elk and bison; Pilot Peak, 11,708 feet.

Teton Wilderness
Location: N.W. Wyoming on the Continental Divide. Access by road to trailheads.
Size: 563,000 acres
Natural Features: Remote, relatively gentle terrain; elk migration through area to Teton Elk Refuge.

Washakie Wilderness
Location: N. Wyoming. Access by road to trailheads.
Size: 714,000 acres
Natural Features: Eighty-mile trail crosses wilderness; Washakie Needles, 12,496 feet; Franks Peak, 13,153 feet, highest peak of the Absaroka Range.

Yellowstone National Park
Location: N.W. corner of Wyoming. Access by five highway entrances; 142-mile figure-eight loop road through park.
Size: 3,400 square miles
Natural Features: The world's largest concentration of geysers, hot springs and related features including Old Faithful Geyser, Grand Prismatic Hot Spring, Steamboat Geyser and Mammoth Hot Springs; richest wildlife preserve in the United States outside of Alaska; Grand Canyon of Yellowstone, 1,200-foot-deep gorge with waterfalls; 700 miles of trails.

Other Wilderness Areas and Wildlife Refuges
Cloud Peak Wilderness Area, Fitzpatrick Wilderness, Mountain Primitive Area, National Elk Refuge, Popo Agie Primitive Area, Whiskey Mountain Primitive Area

A view across part of the Great Sand Dunes of Colorado towards the San Juan Mountains, fifty miles away on the other side of the San Luis Valley.